My name is

____

and I will be the best teacher for my kid

"Crazy Homeschool Mom"

Published by Jade Norton, Susannah Mealove
First Edition, 2024

Cover design by Susannah Mealove

ISBN: 978-83-970304-6-6

Introduction 1

Chapter 1: It's Not Rocket Science 8

Chapter 2: The Levels of Homeschooling 14

Chapter 3: Creating a Classroom 20

Chapter 4: Curriculum Chaos 25

Chapter 5: Customizing Your Curriculum 32

Chapter 6: The Perfect Homeschool Planner 38

Chapter 7: The Daily Schedule 43

Chapter 8: Social Skills 49

Chapter 9: Managing Multiple Ages 53

Chapter 10: Homeschooling Special Needs Children 58

Chapter 11:Homeschooling Through Tough Times 64

Chapter 12: Homeschooling High School 68

Chapter 13: Balancing Work and Homeschooling 74

Chapter 14: Balancing Life and Homeschooling 78

Chapter 15: Finding Your Tribe 82

Chapter 16: Dad's Role 88

Chapter 17: Math Mayhem 92

Chapter 18: Science Experiments 99

Chapter 19: History Lessons 104

Chapter 20: Art Class 109

Chapter 21: Physical Education 116

Chapter 22: Field Trips 124

Chapter 23: Homeschooling on the Road 131

Chapter 24: Grading and Assessments 137

Chapter 25: Celebrating Success 147

Chapter 26: Handling Setbacks 152

Chapter 27: The Day You Decide to Stop 156

Chapter 28: Graduation Day: 160

Chapter 29: What You Learn 163

Introduction: Welcome to the Crazy World of Homeschooling

Greetings from the wonderfully bizarre, amazingly crazy, and wildly unpredictable world of homeschooling! Whether you're just starting out or are knee-deep in the educational profundity, this book serves as your go-to resource for navigating the bumpy, exciting, and frequently terrifying path that is homeschooling your kids. So grab your preferred beverage (extra credit if it's still hot), and let's get started right away!

Homeschooling is, in fact, a fantastic journey filled with amazing discoveries, surprising turns, and—yes—a fair share of mishaps. On some days, you'll feel like you're doing a fantastic job; your students are paying attention, the lectures are flowing, and you might even look nice. Then there will be days when the scientific experiment blows up, the toddler decides trousers are optional, and you wonder if cereal counts as a balanced supper (spoiler alert: it does). Still, it all just makes it more fun!

What to Expect in This Book

Consider this book as your go-to resource for homeschooling survival; it's filled with helpful advice, inspirational tips, and enough of humor to keep you sane throughout the chaotic days.

In this book, you won't find long, continuous texts or strange stories. Its purpose is to provide as much practical knowledge and ideas as possible. Therefore, the following chapters are laid out more in bullet points. This way, you will read this book fairly quickly and won't get bored with unnecessary text.

This is a preview of what's to come:

The Fundamentals: We'll begin by discussing the reasons for homeschooling decisions made by families as well as the fundamental ideas that will steer you through this crazy journey.

Everyday Life: Acquire the skills necessary to organize a homeschooling timetable, manage teaching several age groups, and prevent yourself and everyone else from turning into pumpkins before midday.

Creative Learning: Find out ways to make education engaging and practical, from project-based learning and themed days to make-your-own crafts and spontaneous dance parties. "Shakespeare in the living room," did someone say?

Difficulties and Solutions: We'll address the inescapable difficulties, such as juggling work and teaching and homeschooling through major life transitions, while offering workable answers and a healthy dose of optimism.

Community and Socialization: Since homeschoolers do interact with others, absolutely! We'll explore ways to make sure your children have fulfilling social experiences as well as how to create a community of homeschoolers that encourage and support you.

Special Needs and Individual Differences: We'll discuss how to adapt your approach to suit each child's specific needs, whether they're developing into future Einsteins, have special needs, or simply march to their own beat (figuratively).

Homeschooling While Traveling: You can learn anywhere! Discover how to make every trip an educational adventure by combining homeschooling with travel.

High School and Beyond: Learn how to successfully navigate adolescence, get ready for college, and position your children for success in the future—all without losing your sanity in the process.

Reasons to Start Homeschooling

Families decide to homeschool for a range of reasons, each equally special. You could identify some incentives like these:

Personalized Education: Homeschooling your child allows you to modify the course of instruction to meet his or her specific needs, interests, and learning style. Should your toddler start to fix on dinosaurs, what would happen? Every day paleontology class Just be ready to hear dinosaur roars right at breakfast.

Family Bonding: Homeschooling has unmatched opportunities to strengthen family ties. Like a flour battle in "math" class, which is really baking class, you get to develop and learn and create lifelong events together.

Flexibility and Freedom: You may take vacations when everyone else is locked in school as you are free to pick your own hours. Hello, Disney enjoys off-season trips! Besides, you could find teaching opportunities in unanticipated events.

Safe and Supportive Environment: Homeschooling offers a secure and supportive atmosphere free of the demands and distractions of conventional classrooms. Give up worrying about the mystery meat in the cafeteria or engaging in playground politics.

Cultural and Religious Values: Homeschooling allows you to meaningfully include the cultural, religious, or philosophical beliefs of your family into your child's education. Imagine instructing history from your dinner table while discussing your family's beliefs or background.

Academic Excellence: Homeschooling your child will enable you to provide them a demanding and tailored education that will let them flourish at their own speed. Homeschooling honors their skills whether they are a math genius learning algebra at age nine or a great writer finishing their first novel.

Special Needs: Homeschooling provides specialized assistance and adjustments that regular schools would find difficult to provide for children with exceptional needs. You end up becoming their most dedicated teacher and closest friend.

Experience-Based Learning: Homeschooling becomes the planet your classroom. Real-world interactions—from daily tasks to visits to museums and nature areas—offer amazing learning opportunities. Recall that you used pizza to teach fractions? Wonderful!

Life Transitions: Homeschooling provides the stability and flexibility you need to maintain learning on target, even if spelling lessons have to be done in the car during rush hour. This is true whether your family is changing, you are relocating, adjusting, or simply surviving in your busy life.

Social and Emotional Well-being: Homeschooling provides a safe, motivating atmosphere free from bullying and peer pressure, therefore fostering your child's social and emotional development. They also hang out with their beloved instructor, you!

Homeschool is Not for You If...

As amazing as homeschooling can be, it's not the perfect fit for everyone. Here are a few signs that it might not be your cup of tea:

You Expect Perfection: Homeschooling may be incredibly chaotic and unpredictably messy. If your life revolves around following an exact schedule, you may find it difficult to cope when a peanut butter-covered toddler takes over your well-planned lesson plan.

You're Looking for a Quick Fix: Being a homeschooler is a journey, not a sprint. It calls for patience, time, and effort. In case you're seeking a fast fix for educational difficulties, homeschooling may not be the simple option you seek.

You Don’t Enjoy Being with Your Kids: Having your children at home requires a lot of time commitment. If you can't stand the idea of becoming their lunch lady, principal, and teacher all at once, you should consider your choices.

You're Not Willing to Adapt: The foundation of a successful homeschooling program is flexibility and adaptation. When something isn't working, homeschooling can get frustrating if you're not willing to try something else or adjust your strategy.

You Lack order: Although you don't have to be an exceptionally well-organized ninja, you do need to maintain some degree of order to prevent classes, activities, and everyday routines from becoming disorganized. Homeschooling might be difficult if your idea of order is hiding the remote beneath the sofa.

You Prefer a Structured Environment: The flexible aspect of homeschooling may not be for you if you are someone who needs structure and well-defined boundaries. Some families find comfort in the more regular schedules and routines provided by traditional schools.

You're Not Prepared for the Time Commitment: Homeschooling requires a large time investment. It might not be the greatest choice for your family if you're not willing to put in the required time and effort.

You Have Unrealistic Expectations: You may be disappointed if you think homeschooling would resolve every educational problem or if you anticipate quick results. Being a homeschooler is a journey filled with ups and downs, and your greatest ally is patience.

You Lack Support: If you don't have a support network, homeschooling might be difficult. Taking up the rigors of homeschooling may be more difficult if you don't have the support of friends, family, or the community.

You Don't Want to Learn Everything All the Time: When you homeschool, you frequently learn alongside your child. You may find homeschooling less satisfying if you're not interested in learning new things or maintaining your curiosity.

Homeschooling is a lifestyle decision rather than merely an educational option. It's about setting up a supportive environment where your kids may grow, accepting the freedom to learn together, and taking an open-minded, curious approach to the world. This book will help you navigate the challenging world of homeschooling by providing you with helpful advice, inspirational tales, and lots of laughter.

Chapter 1:
It's Not Rocket Science (Except When It Is)

It's likely that if you've picked up this book, you've either already started homeschooling or are considering it. In any case, we are here to give you confidence: you can succeed!

The Great Myth of Homeschooling

First, let's debunk a common misconception: homeschooling doesn't require a high IQ or a teaching degree. It's not required to speak Latin fluently or understand quantum physics (unless you want to, of course). Creating a learning environment tailored to your child's needs and interests is the goal of homeschooling, as opposed to attempting to mimic the ambiance of a traditional classroom. Yes, there will be days when it seems impossible to keep a herd of cats under control. That is normal.

Think of homeschooling as an ongoing scientific experiment in which you serve as both a scientist and a lab assistant. It is your job to create hypotheses (lesson plans), conduct experiments (tasks and assignments), and assess the findings (the progress of your child). There will be times when your experiments go horribly wrong, but that's an essential part of the learning curve.

Getting Started: The Basics

So, where do you begin? Here are some basic steps to set you on the right path:

Legal Stuff: Don't start until you learn the homeschooling laws in your state. They differ among states, ranging from simple notification to general intent to elaborate paperwork and regular assessments. Ensure compliance with all relevant local regulations so that you are not taken by surprise. Check out the homeschooling associations in the state; they have resources and can give suggestions many times.

Curriculum Choices: Many curriculum options are available for homeschoolers. Everyone has an opportunity to get education whether it is home-based or through formal schooling system. Things can be brought together. Recall that flexibility is one of the key advantages of homeschooling. Examine some programs, talk to other moms who teach their children at home, and choose a curriculum that will both match your teaching style and suit your child's learning preferences best. First use one technique then adjust it if necessary. It is just fine.

Setting Up Your Space: Even if a formal classroom is not necessary, having a dedicated area for studying is beneficial. Discover what works best for your family, whether it's a little sitting place in the living room or a fully equipped school. The idea is to create a space that minimizes outside distractions while increasing comfort and focus. Think about creating several learning zones, such as a tech area, a craft area, and a reading corner. Keep in mind that it doesn't need to be flawless.

Daily Routine: No matter how casual, structure is your friend. Establish a regular routine that includes study time, playing, and relaxation since children learn best when they are consistent. And never lose sight of the fact that it's okay if your day doesn't go as planned. Even in the middle of chaos, things are learned. Make a flexible timetable that suits your family's needs. It might consist of instructional activities in the morning, artistic endeavors at night, and a physical education break in the afternoon. Being adaptable and reliable are both beneficial.

The Role of the Teacher (That's You!)

In addition to being an instructor, you also serve as a coach, counselor, and occasionally a referee. The good news is that no one knows your child like you do. Make the most of that. Adapt your strategy to their preferred mode of learning. Do they learn best visually? Bring out the eye-catching graphs and charts. An experiential learner? Prepare yourself for a plethora of art and scientific projects. You have a responsibility to encourage curiosity and a love of learning in addition to imparting information. Have fun learning new things with one another. It's acceptable to not know every answer. In actuality, accepting the unknown and working together to discover answers may be a really instructive experience for you both.

Handling Doubts and Fears

All homeschooling parents have worries. Will my kids have access to a top-notch education? How will they communicate with other people? Is this correct? Take a deep breath. At-home learning is a journey, not a race. Even though there will be obstacles on your path, perseverance and patience will help you find your groove.

Remember, reaching perfection is not the goal. It is advancement. Celebrate your child's little victories, like mastering a difficult subject or creating something they're proud of. Consider challenges as opportunities to grow as a person. Look for the consolation and encouragement of other homeschooling parents. You're not alone in this place.

Community Support

You are not alone in this. Homeschooling networks, both online and offline, provide an abundance of support and tools. Join local co-ops, engage in online forums, and meet other homeschooling families. Sharing your experiences and recommendations may be very comforting and inspirational. Attend homeschooling conferences, seminars, and meet-ups. These events give excellent opportunity to network, learn new tactics, and form long-lasting connections.

The Fun Factor

Finally, but most essential, remember to have fun. Homeschooling allows you to make lifelong experiences with your kid while also instilling a passion of learning in them. Whether it's a spontaneous field trip to the zoo, a kitchen science experiment that goes horribly wrong, or a leisurely day reading together, these are the moments that define homeschooling.

Include joy and originality in your teaching. Games, puzzles, and hands-on activities may help to make learning more enjoyable. Take advantage of homeschooling's flexibility by investigating things that your kid is interested in. If they're interested by dinosaurs, devote a week to paleontology. If kids like baking, incorporate it into a math and science lesson. The options are limitless.

Common Misconceptions about Homeschooling

Let's clear up some common misunderstandings that may be remaining in your mind.

Socialization: A common misconception regarding homeschooling is that children lose out on socializing. In actuality, homeschooling gives several possibilities for socialization. Homeschooled children often have active social lives, which include co-ops and extracurricular activities, as well as community events and play dates. They also gain from socializing with others of different ages.

Academic Rigor: A common misunderstanding is that homeschooling lacks intellectual rigor. On the contrary, homeschooling enables tailored and accelerated learning. You may personalize the curriculum to your child's strengths and limitations, keeping them challenged and encouraged. Many homeschooling families report that their children achieve much above grade level.

Time Management: Some individuals believe that homeschooling needs an unreasonable amount of time. While it requires devotion, homeschooling may be balanced with other obligations. Effective time management, prioritizing tasks, and incorporating your kid in the planning process may help make it more doable. Remember, the quality of education is more essential than the number of hours.

The First Step is the Hardest

Beginning anything new may be frightening; homeschooling is no exception. The first step is frequently the most difficult, but often the most gratifying. Take it one day at a time and be open about asking help. Experienced homeschoolers abound in a network ready to provide guidance and encouragement.

Keep in mind that each family's homeschooling experience is unique. This is very reasonable as what suits one household might not apply to another. As you negotiate this foreign terrain, treat your child and yourself gently. Errors will happen; they are inevitable but part of the learning process. Accept them, learn from them, and go ahead.

Homeschooling is a road of ups and downs, happiness and tears, challenges and achievements. You and your kid will go on a voyage of exploration. As you begin on this journey, keep in mind that the objective is to foster a love of learning and make meaningful connections, as well as academic accomplishment.

Saddle up then be ready for an adventure. Homeschooling may not be rocket science (until it is), but it is a fascinating adventure filled with discovery, development, and plenty of fun. Good welcome to the club! You've got this, and we're here to support you every step of the way.

Chapter 2: The Levels of Homeschooling: From Preschool to High School – Surviving Each Stage

We will traverse the charming preschool years and the nervous high school years. Every level offers a different set of challenges, successes, and humorous events. virtually completely sane, we will explore the many phases of homeschooling and go through each one with your sanity virtually intact. So get ready, Crazy Homeschool Mama.

Preschool:
The Age of Glitter and Giggles

Greetings from the land of sticky fingers, endless questions, and an inexplicable fixation with glitter. Preschoolers learn via play when they are homeschooled, and the biggest challenge is keeping the paint off the walls (and the dog). It's a beautiful mess.

Art Time: Every day is an art day. And by "art," I mean creating with anything that isn't locked down, such as finger painting and playdough projects. Expect your house to resemble a craft store explosion. Accept it. Keep enough of washing supplies on hand.

Snacktime Mischief: During snack time, learning is just as essential as eating. Use it to teach sharing (good luck with that), colors (what color is the apple?) and counting (how many grapes?).

Incessant Questions: Young children are naturally curious. Expect a barrage of "why" questions. "Why is the blue sky?" "What makes birds sing?" "How come I can't have ice cream for breakfast?" Accept the questions as they are educating you!

Negotiating Nap Time: Getting a preschooler to take a nap may mimic negotiating world peace. Put on your diplomatic hat and remember that a well-rested preschooler is a happy preschooler (and a happy mommy).

Kindergarten: The Age of Wonder and Wiggles

Though joy and wonder abound in kindergarten, it also marks the start of methodical learning. From your active and curious youngsters, you may anticipate a year of grins and wiggles.

Alphabet Adventures: Teaching letters and sounds accounts for a good share of kindergarten. Create fun with games, music, and crafts. It will surprise you how quickly children pick the alphabet while singing it to "Twinkle, Twinkle, Little Star."

Counting Craziness: Every day offers numerical fun. Count everything—from steps to snacks—and use vivid manipulatives to help mathematics seem more relevant. Just be ready for the occasional mistake when counting: "Mom, I can count to ten because I have five fingers on each hand, so that means I can have ten cookies, right?"

Story time: Every day story time helps to foster a love of reading. Give the characters separate voices as your child helps turn the pages. Extra points if they start "reading" back to you from memory their favorite books.

Wiggle Breaks: Young children have a lot of energy. Give them enough wriggle time to keep their attention. One might get great benefit from a tiny dancing party or "Simon Says game".

Elementary School: The Age of Discovery and Doodles

Kids are eager to learn in elementary school, and you have to keep up with their boundless energy and inventiveness. It's a period of exploration. It's also the age at which you begin to notice how much of your own schooling you have forgotten.

Reading Time: It's amazing to see your youngster pick up reading skills. From learning to recognize letters to reading whole sentences, celebrate each accomplishment. & be prepared to hear them recite "Green Eggs and Ham" around 372 times.

Math Adventures: A lot of counting, adding, and subtracting is required in math at this age. Make it enjoyable by utilizing commonplace items, such as measuring ingredients for baking, counting cookies, and multiplying using LEGO bricks.

Scientific Experiments are a kid's favorite kind of scientific learning. Expect a lot of "wow" moments and messy experimentation. Just make sure you always have a sufficient amount of vinegar and baking soda on hand.

Creative Writing: Use enjoyable prompts to inspire creative writing. The tales they come up with will astound you, and perhaps leave you perplexed. "Once upon a time, every assignment was eaten by a dinosaur."

Middle School: The Age of Awkwardness and Awesomeness

Children enter a transitional period in middle school when they become increasingly autonomous and, to be honest, uncomfortable. Accept the oddity and lead them through these years of change.

The Great Social Experiment shows middle school teenagers navigating social dynamics and friendships. Plan group activities and field excursions to assist students develop their social skills and to remind them that life is more than just screens.

Advanced math and eye rolling: As arithmetic develops, eye rolls grow more complex. Show understanding and support. Moreover, be not reluctant to ask teachers, internet resources, or that one buddy who liked mathematics for help.

Science Fair Madness: Middle school students particularly like science fairs. Get ready for late-night creative meetings and challenging assignments. Always have a backup plan ready should the dining room table's baking soda volcano erupt.

Puberty and Pizza: At this age comes puberty. Try for a mood fluctuation, growth spurts, and ravenous appetite. Keep extra pizza and munchies on hand, and be ready for some emotional (and embarrassing) talks.

High School:
The Age of Independence and Intensity

Students in high school are a totally other story. In addition to becoming more independent and ready for the future, they sometimes irritate you. However, it's also exciting to see how wonderful they are becoming into young people. They will be covered in greater detail in the next chapter.

Self-Directed Learning: Students in high school are capable of handling more independent study. Motivate kids to take responsibility for their studies, make objectives, and schedule their time well. This provides you with a little respite and is an excellent preparation for college and beyond.

College Prep: Assist them with every step of the process, from SAT preparation to scholarship applications. Although there is a lot of effort involved, you two will succeed. Remember to enjoy the acceptances as well—this is a tremendous accomplishment!

Driving Instructions: Get ready for the driving instruction. Purchase some stress balls and a decent pair of sunglasses (for all those anxious squints). And never forget that everyone is a newbie at first.

Real-World Skills: Teaching real-world skills in high school is ideal. Skills like cooking, budgeting, and even washing are necessary for future independence. Besides, you could end up with a homemade dinner (or at least less laundry catastrophes).

An incredible and daring experience with great advantages and unique challenges is homeschooling at different educational levels. Every stage, from the glittering preschool years to the rigorous, self-directed high school years, has a special blend of turbulence and delight.

Crazy Homeschool Mama, never stop laughing and appreciating the trip. Your children are being guided through the most formative years of their lives by you really well. Value every moment, laugh at your blunders, and celebrate the little things. Since you will look back and see that it was all worthwhile finally.

Chapter 3: Creating a Classroom: The Kitchen Table vs. The Couch

Okay, you've chosen to attempt homeschooling, and the next step is to set up your classroom. Homeschooling offers the benefit of enabling you to create a space that reflects your family's own style. Making it practical, pleasant, and ready for those inevitable moments of chaos—such as when the scientific experiment turns into a cookery disaster—is critical, whether it's the kitchen table, a soft couch, or even a fancy-pants dedicated classroom.

Finding the Perfect Spot

Before you decide where to park your homeschool HQ, take a good look around your home. Here's how to pick the best spot without sparking a sibling turf war:

Lighting: Everyone stays happier and more alert when there is natural light around (especially those who rise early). Choose a location with plenty of windows if at all possible. Make sure you have adequate lighting if your home seems more like a bat cave than a brightly lighted sanctuary to prevent the feeling of "Why are we doing math in a dungeon?"

Space: You'll need enough space for supplies, books, and maybe a computer or tablet. If you have more than one kid, you may want to set up different areas to reduce distractions. After all, nothing ruins a math lesson more quickly than a fight between siblings over the final crayon.

Comfort: Although using the kitchen table is practical, it's important that your youngster feels comfortable. For the ultimate "I'm learning but it feels like a slumber party" experience, consider bean bags, soft cushions, or ergonomic seats.

Storage: Use shelves, containers, and drawers to keep your materials arranged. Children can concentrate better and switch between "learning time" and "where did all my papers go?" more easily in an area free of clutter.

The Kitchen Table Classroom

The kitchen table is the heart and focus of many families' homeschooling endeavors. It's also where you may convince yourself that cereal counts as a scientific lesson since, after all, calcium is a science. Here's how to utilize this area:

Carry-Along Supplies: Use wheeled carts or caddies to store your stuff. You may effortlessly go from "math class" to "lunch lady" in this way without going insane or tripping over a Lego.
Whiteboard or chalkboard: Set up a small whiteboard or chalkboard next to you to take down notes, scribble notes, or show off your amateur attempts at drawing a mitochondrion. It is a wonderful resource for visual learners and role-playing instructors.
Multipurpose Mats: Consider utilizing placemats or tablecloths as teaching tools. Mats with arithmetic tables, alphabets, and maps may make dinnertime talks about foreign capitals seem extremely normal.

The Cozy Couch Classroom

In case your youngster is more comfortable in a relaxed environment—and who doesn't like a nice sofa session?—the living room might serve as a great place for learning. Here's how to transform your comfortable sofa into an extremely productive machine:

Lap Desks: For using computers and writing, use a robust lap desk. They provide a sturdy surface and are conveniently stowable under the sofa in case your math lesson turns into a power snooze.
Reading Nook: Arrange blankets and pillows to make a comfortable reading nook. Make this your child's favorite location to curl up with a book; they can spend hours lost in Hogwarts or Narnia here without ever having to leave the living room.
Screen Time: Make sure the TV or iPad you're using for instructional films is at a comfortable viewing height and distance (because, let's be honest, Netflix documentaries completely qualify as school). You don't want anybody who binge-watched "Planet Earth" to leave with a sore throat.

Dedicated Classroom

If you have the capacity and want to go all in, setting up a separate homeschool classroom may help establish a clear boundary between "school time" and "home time." Here's how to make it really amazing:

Desk and Chairs: Choose desks and seats depending on the size of your children. Nothing says "serious learning" like a swiveling chair, and adaptable furniture can grow with them.
Adorn: Create a friendly environment using artwork, maps, and teaching materials. Allow your children to help with the decor—after all, who wouldn't want to study in a room decorated with shining stars and motivational quotes like "You can do hard things (like algebra)"?

Supplies Station: Keep everything you need close at hand. Organize books, papers, and craft supplies in labeled bins and shelves. This reduces the need for a daily glue stick scavenger hunt.

Creating a Daily Routine

Maintaining a consistent schedule is very essential to preventing disturbance regardless of the location of your school. Here's how to create a calendar that most days keeps everyone on target:

Create a consistent morning schedule: Breakfast, some yoga or stretching (yes, "Mom's coffee dance"), and a review of the day agenda may all fall here. It sets a nice tone and aids in the elimination of the morning blahs.

Academic blocks: Sort the day into little chunks. Alternately between classes and stop to keep your child engaged and prevent brain overload. Think "math sprint," then "snack marathon."

Flexible schedule: Although planning is important, flexibility is very vital. Should your child be having a difficult day or should you find out that today's physics class involves an unannounced "gravity test" with the cat, be ready to adjust. Change and keep going.

Review sessions: help you to wrap up the day. Talk about what went well, what needs more work, and what everyone is looking forward. It's a great way to finish the day and, to be honest, arrange how the scientific experiment tomorrow should go.

Making It Work for You

Recall that there isn't a one, effective method for homeschooling. Establishing a schedule and atmosphere that work for your particular family dynamics is the aim. Don't be scared to try new things and adjust as necessary. Your kids will feel more engaged in the process and may even come up with some really great suggestions (like "Tuesday Pajama Day").

Chapter 4: Curriculum Chaos: Choosing the Right Path (or Paths!)

You've set up your homeschool area, which may be a designated classroom, the kitchen table, or a comfortable sofa. The exciting (and sometimes daunting) part is here: selecting your program. Imagine that you are choosing the foundational materials of your child's education, rather than clothing for a formal occasion. One size does not fit all, just as in the world of fashion.

Understanding Your Options

You must understand the many educational philosophies before you go into the vast sea of homeschooling materials. This is a synopsis to get you here:

Traditional Curriculum: Using textbooks, workbooks, and a linear course of instruction, this approach adheres to a conventional school model. See it as a classy, classic outfit.

Classical education: Emphasizing the trio—grammar, logic, and rhetoric—this approach promotes critical thinking as well as outstanding literary creations. It's like the polished, scholarly tweed jacket and elbow patches of education.

The ideas of Charlotte Mason center nature study, storytelling, and living books. It's all about inspiring a desire of learning from rich, interesting material. Think of it as creative, bohemian clothing with plenty of layers and textures.

Montessori: By use of self-directed activities and hands-on experiences, Montessori education fosters independence and practical skills. Think of it as the basic, practical clothes that nevertheless looks great.

Unschooling: Under a learner-led approach known as "unschooling," the child's interests and natural curiosity come first over a planned course. It's the intellectual equivalent of wearing whatever you want, whenever you want: comfort over convention.

Unit Studies: Six unit studies combine several disciplines around a single problem. It's like a mix-and-match wardrobe, with everything exactly synchronized.

Hybrid: Sometimes homeschooling families mix elements from several ideas to create a customized method.

This is the instructional smorgasbord—a little bit of everything to suit your tastes.

The Great Curriculum Hunt

Having a rudimentary awareness of the many ideologies now can help you begin your search for the correct course of study. These ideas should help you negotiate the process:

Know Your Child's Learning Style: Find out whether your youngster learns best visually and like images and diagrams. Alternatively they may be kinesthetic learners, meaning they must move and touch something to grasp. Your curriculum may be much improved by matching it to your child's learning style. It all comes down to what makes people comfortable, just as when deciding between a fashionable jacket and a cosy sweater.

Set Your Goals: This year what do you want your kid to accomplish? Having well defined objectives will enable you to reduce your options. Whether your goals are learning multiplication or delving deeply into ancient history, clarity is essential. Consider it like choosing a dress for a certain occasion; you have to know where you would dress correctly.

Budget Issues: Homeschooling is not financially burdensome. There are many of reasonably priced (and even free) materials at hand.

Sort your priorities based on your realistic expenditure range. It's like discovering a fantastic garment on sale; you don't have to shell out a bunch to look amazing.

Choose a curriculum: find one which lets you make necessary changes in flexibility and adaptability. Children develop and evolve as well as their educational requirements. It is very useful to be able to change your strategy without having to start again. It's like having a wardrobe with adaptable items suitable for both dressing up and down.

Get Recommendations and Reviews: Ask other homeschooling parents for their wisdom. Gold mines of knowledge include online forums, neighborhood co-ops, and homeschooling organizations. Consider it as asking your fashionable buddy where they found their incredible shoes; personal suggestions are usually the finest.

Curriculum Choices

Let's take a look at some specific curriculum options that align with different educational philosophies:

1. **Traditional Curriculum:**
   - **Abeka**: Known for its rigorous and structured approach, Abeka offers comprehensive programs from kindergarten through high school. It's like the tailored suit of curricula – reliable and polished.

- **Saxon Math**: A highly regarded math program that emphasizes incremental learning and practice. Think of it as the sturdy, dependable pair of jeans that fit just right.

2. **Classical Education:**
   - **The Well-Trained Mind**: This resource by Susan Wise Bauer provides a detailed guide for classical education at home. It's like the classic little black dress – timeless and essential.
   - **Story of the World**: Also by Susan Wise Bauer, this series makes history come alive through engaging narratives. It's like a beautifully crafted accessory that adds flair to any outfit.

3. **Charlotte Mason:**
   - **Ambleside Online**: A free, online curriculum based on Charlotte Mason's principles, featuring a rich selection of living books. It's the boho-chic collection you can mix and match.
   - **Simply Charlotte Mason**: Offers guides, book lists, and resources to help you implement the Charlotte Mason method. It's like having a personal stylist for your homeschool.

4. **Montessori:**
   - **Montessori by Mom**: Monthly subscription boxes with hands-on materials and activities based on Montessori principles. It's like a surprise fashion box that delivers new outfits to your door.

- **North American Montessori Center (NAMC)**: Provides comprehensive Montessori training and curriculum guides. It's the capsule wardrobe of education – minimalistic and effective.

5. **Unschooling:**
   - **John Holt's Books**: Pioneering unschooling advocate John Holt's books, like "How Children Learn," offer inspiration and guidance. It's the DIY fashion approach – create your own style.
   - **Unschooling.com**: A wealth of resources, articles, and community support for unschooling families. It's like having a network of fashion bloggers sharing their best tips.

6. **Unit Studies:**
   - **Five in a Row**: Uses classic children's books as the basis for unit studies that cover multiple subjects. It's the educational equivalent of a themed wardrobe – cohesive and fun.
   - **Konos Curriculum**: Hands-on, character-based unit studies that integrate various subjects. It's like a mix-and-match set that keeps everything coordinated.

Making Your Choice

Choosing a curriculum might be difficult with so many options. These final hints will help you come to an answer:

Trial and Error: One should not hesitate to try; mistakes are inevitable. Try everything; then, determine it is not for you. Among the many benefits of homeschooling is flexibility. Think of it like dressing: sometimes you have to try many combinations before you get the proper fit.

Ask help: Consult more seasoned homeschoolers right away. Their comments might be really useful and assist to avoid certain errors. Learning from someone who has already nailed the appearance a fashion advice is like that.

Trust Your Feelings: You should parent your child most suitably. Based on your gut instinct, choose anything that appears fit for your family. If a curriculum makes one pleased and inquisitive, it is most certainly a great choice. Remember that this is your own homeschool road; treat it as such and as different as your chosen attire.

Choosing a curriculum sets your homeschooling path in an intriguing new direction. This is an opportunity to customize your child's education to fit their needs and interests, therefore producing a really unique learning environment. Remember also that there is no right or wrong option; only what fits your family will make sense.

Chapter 5: Customizing Your Curriculum: Tailoring Learning to Fit Like a Glove

Customizing the curriculum to match your child's interests and learning style is one of the biggest benefits of homeschooling. It fits like a glove and looks amazing, exactly like a custom suit designed for you. But instead of fabric, we have to deal with projects, books, and perhaps some glitter explosions. We'll look at ways to personalize your curriculum in this chapter to maximize learning effectiveness and engagement.

Understanding Learning Styles

Every child has a unique way of learning. Here's a quick overview of the main learning styles and how to cater to each:

Visual Learners: For these children, visual learning is more effective. Consider using charts, graphs, and vibrant notes. They are the ones that can create a great color-coding scheme out of a simple arithmetic worksheet. Make great use of mind maps, infographics, and plenty of graphic aids. Urge them to sketch their own pictures and diagrams. Just be ready for your home to seem like an art exhibition of instructional posters.

Auditory Learners: Sound is all these students find appealing. They pick knowledge by speaking and listening. It will be they that will teach their toy animals mathematics. Add oral presentations, audiobooks, and debates to customize your work. Let them walk you or a sibling through ideas. Get a decent set of headphones for your sanity and audiobooks.

Kinesthetic learners: those who must move and do—have particular challenges. Physical interaction and practical exercises enable kids to learn most effectively. It is they who may transform a scientific experiment into a tiny science fair. Add movement-based learning, constructing projects, and experiments. Plan regular pauses for physical exercise. Should your living room become a temporary lab or building site, you should not be startled.

Learners in Reading and Writing: These students gain knowledge mostly by reading and writing. It is they who could document their experiences with homeschooling. Offer plenty of literature, writing projects, and chances for journaling. Urge them to write their own reports and tales. Stock notebooks and pencils; you will need them.

Incorporating Interests

Including your child's interests in their studies may make them value learning more. This is how you do it:

Interest-Based Projects: Assemble projects around your children's areas of interest.

If kids are particularly interested in dinosaurs, create a unit study on paleontology. Take them farther into astronomy if they have a fascination with space. You can find yourself knee-deep in dinosaur skeletons or shooting handmade rockets.

Passion-Driven Research: Permit your children to choose the topics for their own research projects. This fosters independence and a love of learning. Just be prepared to take on some unusual study topics, like the life cycle of the dung beetle.

Themed Weeks: Based on your child's interests, plan their themed weeks. A week-long program named "Under the Sea" may include marine biology teaching, virtual aquarium tours, and crafts with an ocean theme. Perhaps the next is "Space Exploration," which involves astronaut training (a.k.a. trampoline jumping).

Real-World Applications: Make connections between theoretical subjects and useful applications. If your child likes to cook, include history (recipe origins), math (measured components), and science (chemical reactions). The nicest part is that you can taste the finished product! Win-win!

Creating Flexibility in Your Curriculum

Adaptability is necessary for curriculum customization. Here's how to remain flexible:

Modular Learning: Use interchangeable modular learning components. This allows you to easily switch topics based on your child's level of engagement and interest. Consider it a feast of information, with a little bit of everything.

Choice Boards: Create choice boards with many tasks and assignments for each subject. Allow your child to select which ones to finish. It makes them feel more in control and may renew their desire. It also resembles a game show.

Adaptable Scheduling: Do not be afraid to deviate from the plan. Allow your child to complete a project if they are really invested in it. If one subject isn't compelling, try another. Recalculating is OK while homeschooling; it's equivalent to using a GPS for travel.

Seasonal Learning: Tailor your course of study to the shifting of the seasons. Learn about astronomy in the winter, oceanography in the summer, and flora and weather in the spring. Seasonal themes may make learning seem fresh and current.

Making Customization Fun

Personalization should be pleasant rather than a chore. Here are some suggestions to keep it fun:

DIY Learning materials: Create your own instructional materials. Make your own educational videos, board games, and even flashcards. It's an excellent chance to utilize your ideas to design instructional materials that are uniquely tailored to your child.

Learning Challenges: Provide competitions and learning opportunities. Who can build the tallest tower with just toothpicks and marshmallows? Who can come up with the funniest tale using every spelling term? It's remarkable how a little competition can energize the learning process.

Field Trip Fun: Plan your trips around the themes covered in your curriculum. Are you a geology student? Explore a local cave or rock construction. Researching the past? Visit a historical site. Scavenger hunts and photo opportunities may transform routine excursions into exciting events.

Themed Learning Days: Plan learning sessions around a common subject for all of the products. Treasure hunts, pirate-themed math puzzles, and the recital of pirate stories may all be part of "Pirate Day." Just prepare to shout a lot of "Arrr!"

Funny Situations in Customized Learning

Customizing may lead to some rather humorous events. These will make you laugh.

The Dinosaur Enthusiast: Your child's passion for dinosaurs is so intense that it turns every subject into a lesson on them. "Can we work T-Rex math, Mom?" Suddenly you're looking for the weight of a Stegosaurus instead of simply basic fractions.

The Space Cadet: Your child is keen about dressing in an astronaut suit to every session after a week of space-themed instruction. You come across explaining grammatical rules to an explorer sporting a helmet.

The Little Chef: During a cooking lesson, your child decides to play around with spices. The last meal is... unique. "Well, that's rather creative—I've never had spaghetti flavored with cinnamon before!"

The garden Explorer: An outdoor biology lesson becomes a full-fledged adventure as your child notes every bug and plant in the garden. By the end, your kitchen table is covered with a range of "specimens."

Making your curriculum fit your child's interests and chosen learning style can help homeschooling be more effective and appealing. Knowing your child's learning style, considering their interests, and keeping things fun and flexible can help you create a tailored learning environment as special as they are.

Chapter 6: The Perfect Homeschool Planner: Your Trusty Notebook Sidekick

Let's give the homeschool planner some recognition as the unsung hero of home education. This amazing notebook is your lifeline, your brain in a book, and sometimes the only thing keeping everything from falling apart. Not just any notebook, either—this is your trustworthy companion, your go-to organizer, and sometimes your stress reliever (when you scribble furiously all over it). Inspired by top planners, let's explore the delightfully bizarre world of designing the ideal homeschool planner.

Motivated by the best planners out there, let's go into the wonderfully bizarre realm of creating the perfect homeschool planner.

The Anatomy of the Perfect Planner

Creating the ideal homeschool planner is similar to putting together the greatest superhero; it must be strong, adaptable, and able to save the day. The following should be included in your ideal planner:

The Cover: This is your planner's outfit. Let's start with the cover. It must be strong, resilient, and—let's be honest—gorgeously ornamented. Consider using bold hues, motivational sayings, and maybe even some glitter (if you're courageous enough to handle the cleanup). You'll be seeing it a lot, so it should make you grin every time you see it.

The Calendar: The calendar is the central component of any planner. Weekly spreads are necessary to organize the minute details, while monthly spreads are necessary to grasp the larger picture. Remember to provide plenty of space for notes; you'll need it for anything from reminders about upcoming field trips to reminders to "remember to buy more coffee."

Lesson Plans: The real magic occurs in this area. Divide up your topics, make a to-do list, and allow time for those spur-of-the-moment lessons (such as when your child decides they must know all there is to know about llamas). Since homeschooling seldom goes as planned, make sure to include a section for backup plans.

To-Do Lists: The sidekick of your trusted companion is the to-do list. Thanks to your unexpected interest in knights and castles, these lists help you stay organized with anything from "buy more glue sticks" to "research medieval weaponry." As there is nothing more fulfilling than crossing off a job as accomplished, be sure to add checkboxes.

Meal Planner: Let's face it, organizing meals and homeschooling go hand in hand. Make sure to include sections for shopping lists, weekly meal planning, and emergency takeaway numbers. You and your children both know that you cannot instruct when hungry.

Field Trip diary: Use a field trip diary to keep track of all those incredible educational excursions. Add the location, the date, and the knowledge you gained. It's a wonderful opportunity to reflect on the past and recall that one occasion when you transformed a simple grocery shop excursion into an extensive economics lecture.

Attendance Tracker: It's a good idea to monitor attendance even if you're homeschooling. Note who was there, who was "sick," and who was "mentally absent" (we've all had such days) in this area.

Grades and Progress: This section is for you if you maintain grades. Monitor achievements, grades, and advancement. Honor the successes and identify the areas that need a little more attention. Recall that everyone receives an A+ for their efforts!

Goal-setting: Set aside time in this section to discuss and monitor your objectives. These might be objectives related to school, personal growth, or even family. It's an excellent method to maintain motivation and concentrate.

Reading Log: Maintain a record of every book you and your children read. Provide the book's title, author, and a brief summary of your thoughts on it.

It's a fun method to track your reading progress for the year and to inspire a passion for reading.

Extracurricular Activities: Remember to keep track of extracurricular activities such as clubs, athletics, and music courses. This guarantees that you don't double-book violin practice with soccer matches and lets you see the comprehensive education your children are receiving.

Thoughts and Notes: Make sure to provide enough of area for thoughts and notes. Having a special place for these ideas is priceless, whether it's a fantastic new teaching technique you've learned about, a quotation that motivated you, or a reminder to purchase extra post-it notes.

List of Contacts: Make a list of all the people you need to get in touch with, such as other homeschooling parents, tutors, and local resources. In this manner, assistance or guidance is never more than a phone call away.

Borrowed Books and Supplies: Keep track of all borrowed materials to ensure nothing disappears. Include areas in your calendar for due dates and who borrowed what; it's like having your own little library system.

Homeschooling Budget: Set aside money in your budget specifically for homeschooling. Keep tabs on your spending, create plans for upcoming purchases, and confirm that you are according to your budget.

Password Tracker: Maintain a safe area where you can keep track of the passwords to all those websites and online resources that provide education. No more losing track of the math game website you signed up for with an animal motif!

Personalizing Your Planner

Your own style and personality should come through in your homeschool planner. To really make it yours, try these suggestions:

Color-Coding: Invest in a rainbow-colored set of highlighters and pencils. Sort topics, events, and even emotions using color coding. Purple represents those rare but wonderful "everything went perfectly" days, red represents "oh my gosh, why won't this child listen" days, and green represents pleasant days.

Doodles and Stickers: Add some excitement to your calendar by using stickers and doodling. Put a cheerful face sticker on finished projects, a star sticker on excellent work, and maybe a "keep going" sticker on difficult days. When you're bored or have an idea, scribble in the margins—after all, this is your calendar.

Motivational Phrases: Incorporate motivational phrases to stay inspired. It's always a good idea to remember that coffee is your buddy and that "You've got this, Mama!" Include sayings from your children as well; sometimes they have unexpectedly funny and insightful statements.

Your homeschool planner is your companion on your homeschooling journey; it's more than simply a notepad. It maintains your sanity (mainly), motivation, and organization. It serves as a space for goals, aspirations, and the odd doodling. So go ahead and live the planner life, customize it to your liking, and make it your reliable travel partner.

Chapter 7: The Daily Schedule: When Pajamas Become School Uniforms

You've chosen the ideal curriculum and organized your homeschool area. It's time to start working on one of the most challenging aspects of homeschooling: developing a daily schedule. If your schedule is flawlessly planned out with no bumps in the road, you may want to slightly reduce your expectations. Homeschooling is not so much a leisurely sail as it is a rollercoaster. However, you can develop a rhythm that works for your family with a little forethought, adaptability, and humor.

Morning Madness

Given that the day starts in the morning, let's begin there. It might be difficult to get everyone ready in the morning, particularly if there is a "night owl" attitude in your home. To control the morning chaos, try these suggestions:

Regular Wake-Up Time: Make an effort to rise at the same time every day. This helps everyone get on the same schedule and establish a habit. Yes, even if it means using a timer on the coffee maker, it includes you.

Daily Routine: Establish a basic daily schedule that consists of breakfast, dressing, and a brief workout. Kind of like a mental warm-up. One morning, the family and I attempted a family yoga practice. Needless to say, the cat had the finest downward dog.

Morning Meeting: Call a brief meeting of all parties to go over the schedule for the day. Everyone is brought up to speed and expectations are established thanks to this. We refer to it as "homeroom," and I generally have a second cup of coffee while the kids drink hot chocolate together.

Academic Blocks: The Core of the Day

After you've made it through the daily grind, it's time to focus on your studies. Organizing your time for academic purposes might help you stay on course.

Time Blocking: Allocate specific chunks of time throughout the day for each topic. For instance, science in the afternoon, language arts before to lunch, and math in the morning. It resembles a schedule from school, without the bell.

Focused Learning: Avoid distractions and concentrate only on one topic throughout each block. If necessary, set a timer to help everyone stay on target. We use a tomato-shaped kitchen timer because nothing shouts "time to focus" like a ticking vegetable.

Breaks: Schedule frequent pauses so that everyone has an opportunity to stretch, eat, and rest. Imagine it like recess, but with more goodies and less regulations. Our "dance break" playlist has five minutes of upbeat music that is guaranteed to improve focus.

Hands-on Activities: Incorporate practical projects and activities to break up the monotony. Cooking, art projects, and science experiments may all be excellent opportunities to learn by doing. We've had our fair share of baking soda volcanoes in our kitchen, so be ready for a little mess.

Lunch and Learn

Taking a break from formal classes and embracing pleasurable, informal learning may be best done over lunchtime. Here's some suggestions:

Educational Videos: During lunch, watch a documentary or instructive film.

It's a clever way of learning as you eat. After seeing a space documentary, we had lunch and discussed black holes and space travel.

Read-Aloud Time: While everyone is eating, discuss a great book. It's a pleasant way to enjoy literature with one another. We're now going through a classic adventure series; nothing beats some swashbuckling to liven up a boring PB&J.

Discussion Time: Use lunchtime to discuss the things you've already learned as well as those you still need to cover. This is also a wonderful chance to discuss any questions or concerns. It's also an excellent excuse to stay late for dessert.

Afternoon Adventures

In the afternoon, there may be a mix of extracurricular activities, leisure time, and continuing education. Here's how to keep momentum:

Project Time: Set aside the afternoon for more intricate tasks that need more focus and time. This might be a historical project, a scientific experiment, or an artwork. We once spent a week in the dining room creating a solar system model. It was a worldwide success.

Outdoor Learning: Take your classes outside when the weather allows. Outdoor activities, such as gardening and nature walks, may be both stimulating and educational.

Our outdoor treasure hunt is an annual favorite since it never gets tired seeking for "something squishy."

Extracurricular Activities: Set aside the afternoon for sports, music courses, or other extracurricular activities. It's an excellent way to blend personal interests with academic work. We've had impromptu soccer games and violin recitals in our living room.

Independent Work: Allow your children to work on their own projects for a time. This develops self-control and time management skills. We call this "quiet time" when everyone goes about their business (and I sneak in some reading).

Evening Wind-Down: As the day winds down, it's important to transition from school mode to relaxation mode. Here are some tips to end the day on a high note:

Review and Reflect: Take some time to reflect on the day's work and what you accomplished. Rejoice in the victories and talk about the obstacles. We have what we term a "family debrief" and cookies are usually included.

Relax with some peaceful reading time: This might take the form of a family read-aloud or solo reading. A "book nook" section adorned with plush blankets and cushions awaits you—ideal for unwinding with a good book as the sun goes down.

Family Time: Take some time to bond with your loved ones. Have a movie night, play a board game, or just talk about what happened today.

You may unwind and reconnect in this wonderful manner. One of our favorites recently was a weekly "game night"—we learned that a game of Monopoly can be very fierce.

Create a Relaxing Nighttime Routine: This will help everyone unwind. Some examples of this include a long, hot bath, soft music, and a tale before bed. We always tell "two truths and a tall tale" as a custom - it's incredible how imaginative tales can get at bedtime.

Creating a daily routine for homeschooling is all about finding what works best for your family. It's a balance of structure and flexibility, academics and fun, and a healthy dose of patience and humor. Remember, every day won't be perfect, and that's okay. The goal is to create a learning environment that's engaging, supportive, and enjoyable for everyone involved.

Chapter 8:
Social Skills: Playdates, Co-ops, and Online Friends

Although homeschooling is an amazing path of education and development, even the most committed homeschool family must sometimes go out into the outside world. Extracurricular activities and socialization are essential for a well-rounded education. Now, let's explore how to maintain our trademark wacky homeschool mother humor while making sure your kids have plenty of fun and interaction.

The Importance of Socialization

Unlike what the general public believes, homeschoolers do not spend their whole day alone, curled over books. In fact, one of the best parts of homeschooling is often socializing. Here are some tips to ensure your kid is interacting with others enough:

Join a Homeschool Group: Homeschool groups provide chances for frequent get-togethers, field excursions, and cooperative education. They also provide you the opportunity to commiserate with other parents of homeschooling children. Consider it a kind of support group where everyone knows how difficult it may be to explain fractions to others.

Playdates and Park Days: Organizing regular playdates and park days helps youngsters meet new people and get some energy out. Just keep in mind that a two-hour park visit apparently necessitates a buffet, so bring extra food.

Community courses: Enroll your kids in courses related to sports, music, dance, or the arts. It's a great opportunity for them to meet children who share their interests and pick up new skills. It also provides you with a respite for some much-needed "me time"—or, let's face it, a sleep.

Extracurricular Activities: Finding the Right Fit

Participating in extracurricular activities is essential to a well-rounded education. They provide children the chance to discover their hobbies, hone their abilities, and form connections. Here are a few well-liked choices:

Sports Teams: Sports teams, whether they play basketball, soccer, or swimming, are excellent for cooperation and physical conditioning. Just be ready for the never-ending cycle of having to wash jerseys and discovering lost soccer balls in the most unusual locations.

Scouting and Youth organizations: Social activities, skill development, and community service are all combined in programs like Scouts and other youth organizations. They also include stylish clothes and badges, and who doesn't like a beautiful badge?

Music and the Arts: Kids may express themselves and grow creatively via the arts, which range from piano instruction to theater groups. And simply refer to the collection of incomplete art pieces in your living room as a "exhibition."

STEM groups: For aspiring scientists and engineers, robotics, coding, and scientific groups are ideal. Just be prepared for a home full of electronic devices and the odd explosion (preferably of the scientific type).

Balancing Socialization and Academics

Finding a good balance between social activities and academic study may be difficult. Here are some suggestions to keep things going smoothly:

Schedule Wisely: Create a weekly calendar that balances academics and extracurricular activities. Use a calendar to keep track of everything because, let's face it, no one wants to be the parent who forgets it's "Crazy Hair Day" at dance.

Set priorities: Help your youngster pick activities that pique their interest rather than overburdening their calendar with too many obligations. Quality wins out over quantity, unless it's chocolate, in which case more is better.

Flexible Learning: Take advantage of homeschooling's flexibility for learning. If there is a large soccer event coming up, make adjustments to your academic calendar. Remember that learning occurs everywhere, not just at the kitchen table.

Socialization Myths and Realities

Homeschoolers Are Socially Awkward: Homeschoolers are generally well-adjusted and socially competent, contrary to a common misconception. They mingle with individuals of different ages and enjoy several social activities. Have you lately met a teenager? Awkwardness is not limited to homeschooling.

Homeschoolers Have No Friends: Homeschoolers have a varied range of friends from various activities and areas, contrary to a common misconception. Furthermore, kids do not have to cope with the drama of school cliques. Friendship without the cafeteria politics - sounds lovely, right?

Homeschoolers Do Not Attend Proms: In reality, many homeschool organizations plan their own proms, dances, and social gatherings. If everything else fails, who says you can't have a prom in your living room? Anyone up for some DIY decorations?

Socialization and extracurricular activities are critical to a well-rounded homeschooling experience. They provide possibilities for study, camaraderie, and plenty of fun. You may assure your child's academic and social success by striking the correct balance and maintaining a sense of humor.

Chapter 9: Managing Multiple Ages: Teaching Kids from Toddlers to Teens

If you thought homeschooling one kid was difficult, consider educating numerous children of varying ages at the same time. It's similar to operating a one-room schoolhouse, only your pupils may also be siblings who argue often. But don't panic; with a few methods, a little patience, and a decent sense of humor, you can keep everyone learning while remaining quite calm.

Understanding the Challenges

Homeschooling several ages has its own unique set of obstacles. Here are some typical concerns you may encounter:

Diverse Learning Needs: Every kid has unique learning styles and paces. While one person may breeze through multiplication, another may struggle with simple addition.

Time Management: Balancing time with children may be challenging. You want to give each kid the attention they need without disregarding others.

Resource Sharing: Limited resources might create problems. Who gets to use the computer during their online class? Whose turn is it to utilize the markers in their art project?

Sibling Dynamics: Learning with siblings may be both beneficial and challenging. They may inspire and distract or compete with one another.

Strategies for Success

Group Learning: To educate many kids at once, integrate topics wherever you can. Read-aloud, science, and history are excellent subjects for group education. Adapt exercises to varying skill levels while maintaining a common core curriculum. For example, older children may write essays while learning ancient Egypt, while smaller children can sketch pyramids.

Individualized Learning Plans: Based on each child's age, aptitude, and interests, create a unique learning plan for them. This guarantees that each person is suitably challenged and kept interested. To monitor the development and objectives of every kid, use planners or checklists.

Rotating Schedules: Create a timetable that rotates so you can give each kid concentrated attention while the others work on their own. You may do this in 30-minute periods, for example, rotating through each kid.

Buddy System: For certain activities, pair older and younger kids. This promotes mentoring and camaraderie in addition to helping with time management. Older children may support their own learning while providing you with a respite by helping with basic arithmetic or reading.

Educational Games and Apps: Keep one youngster busy while you work with another by using educational games and apps. These are an excellent resource for personal study time as they may be entertaining as well as instructive.

Flexible Curriculum: Select a curriculum that is adaptable and flexible. Certain curricula are designed especially for teaching across many age groups, providing varying degrees of intricacy for the same subject.

Project-Based Learning: Introduce project-based learning, allowing kids of all ages to participate to the best of their abilities. Science investigations, model construction, and presentation creation are just a few examples of project types. All kids are able to take on projects appropriate for their ability.

Daily Quiet Time: Establish a daily quiet period during which each person reads on their own or does other quiet activities. This allows you to take a break and guarantees that every youngster learns how to study alone.

Outsource When Required: Don't be scared to contract out some tasks or topics. Tutors, nearby co-ops, and online courses may all provide further knowledge and assistance.

Self-Care for the Teacher: Taking care of many kids may be quite taxing. To prevent burnout, make sure you schedule time for self-care. Plan frequent breaks, engage in enjoyable activities, and ask other parents who homeschool for assistance.

Creating a Balanced Routine

A well-rounded schedule is essential for overseeing many kids. This is an example of a daily planner that uses a variety of techniques:

Morning Meeting: To go over the agenda for the day and establish objectives, start with a family meeting.

Group Learning Block: Take part in a read-aloud or historical lecture as a group.
Individual Work Block 1: As you assist the younger kid with reading, the older child works on arithmetic on their own.

Break Time: Snacks and outdoor playtime are provided for everyone during this break.

Individual Work Block 2: Now that you are in a different position, assist the larger kid with their writing while the younger one engages in educational games or puzzles.

Lunch and Learn: Share a meal while watching a teaching film or having a conversation about a current issue.

Project Time: Assist each kid in accordance with their capacity by involving them in a practical project.

Quiet Time: Everyone gets their own time for individual study or quiet reading.

Extracurricular Activities: Practice your sport, music, or other activities in the afternoon.

Review and Reflect: Summarize the day's lessons and discuss any successes or setbacks.

Dealing with Conflicts

Sibling rivalry is unavoidable, particularly while studying alongside one another. Here are some pointers for handling disputes and maintaining harmony:

Establish Clear Expectations: Specify guidelines and standards for conduct in the classroom. Having clear rules in place helps stop many problems before they ever arise.

Conflict Resolution Skills: Instruct your kids on how to resolve conflicts. Playing through several situations may be an enjoyable and productive approach to get experience.

Separate Spaces: Having areas for each youngster to work alone might be helpful when tensions escalate. Often, a change of location helps calm a heated argument.

Positive Reinforcement: To promote cooperative conduct, use positive reinforcement. Honor cooperation and emphasize the advantages of collaboration.

Scheduled Breaks: Make sure to include plenty of downtime for unwinding. Exercise has been shown to lower stress and improve mood.

Although homeschooling children of different ages might often seem like herding cats, it is totally feasible to have a peaceful and effective learning atmosphere if you use the appropriate techniques. Accept the mess, smile at the mistakes, and keep in mind that learning together is more important than perfection.

Chapter 10: Homeschooling Special Needs Children: Embracing Uniqueness and Finding Joy in the Journey

Homeschooling special needs children brings both unique obstacles and amazing opportunities. It demands patience, ingenuity, and a thorough awareness of your child's requirements. However, it also provides the freedom to personalize teaching to their individual strengths and problems. In this chapter, we'll look at ways for building a friendly and successful learning environment for special needs children, with lots of humor to keep things lighthearted.

Understanding Your Child's Needs

The first step in homeschooling a special needs kid is to identify their individual requirements. Here is how to start:

Professional Assessments: Seek expert examinations to better understand your child's requirements. This might involve examinations from physicians, psychologists, or educational professionals. It paints a clear picture of strengths, problems, and required modifications.

Individualized Education Plan: Create an Individualized Education Plan (IEP) based on your child's requirements. Outline your objectives, methods, and adjustments. Review and update it on a frequent basis to ensure that it continues to fit your child's changing requirements.

Observation and Flexibility: Consider your child's learning style and adapt your approach accordingly. What works one day may not work the next, and that's OK. Adaptability is critical.

Creating a Supportive Learning Environment

Calm and Orderly Space: Create a peaceful and organized learning environment. Reduce clutter and distractions. Soft lighting, comfy seating, and a few cherished things may all contribute to an appealing atmosphere.

Routine and Structure: Develop a constant schedule and organization. Predictability helps to minimize anxiety and increase concentration. Use visual timetables and timers to stay on track.

Sensory Accommodations: Provide sensory accommodations as required. This might offer noise-cancelling headphones, fidget tools, or a quiet area for breaks. Know your child's sensory triggers and preferences.

Positive Reinforcement: Use positive reinforcement to promote improvement. Recognize efforts and appreciate little triumphs. A reward system might be motivational, such as stickers, more playtime, or a favorite food.

Customizing the Curriculum

Multi-Sensory Learning: Use multi-sensory learning exercises. Use images, hands-on activities, and audio materials. For tactile learning, use sandpaper letters, or teach arithmetic concepts with songs.

Breaks and Movement: Schedule frequent breaks and include exercise into sessions. Short, frequent breaks help you stay focused. Incorporate movement into the learning process, such as dancing through arithmetic problems or acting out historical courses.

Technology & Tools: Use technology and assistance tools. Educational applications, speech-to-text software, and interactive whiteboards may all help students study more effectively.Just be prepared for a few technical glitches - "Mom, why is the iPad speaking in Spanish?"

Interest Based Learning: Make learning more exciting for your youngster by tapping into his or her passions. If kids like trains, include them in arithmetic problems or reading tasks. Passion-driven learning motivates them.

Incorporating Therapies

Speech Therapy: Incorporate speech therapy activities into everyday courses. Practice your pronunciation, vocabulary, and conversational abilities. Make it enjoyable by playing games and acting out scenarios.

Occupational Therapy: Occupational therapy include tasks to improve fine motor skills, coordination, and sensory integration. This might be anything from stringing beads to playing with playdough.

Behavioral Therapy: Utilize behavioral therapy strategies to address difficulties. Use tactics such as positive reinforcement, clear expectations, and consistent penalties.

Physical Therapy: Add physical therapy exercises to your regimen. Stretching, balancing activities, and strength exercises may all be included into playtime or outdoor activities.

Building a Support Network

Support Groups: Assemble a support group comprised of parents of children with special needs. Exchange of tactics and experiences may be quite beneficial. It's also comforting to know that you're not alone.

Expert Assistance: Collaborate with experts who comprehend your child's requirements. Doctors, therapists, and special education instructors may all provide helpful advice and resources.

Family and Friends: Never be afraid to ask for support from your loved ones. Family assistance, whether it takes the form of babysitting, running errands, or simply lending a sympathetic ear, may make a big impact.

Online groups: Take part in forums and online groups for homeschooling students with special needs. These may provide guidance, materials, and emotional support from parents going through comparable difficulties.

Encouraging Social Interaction

Social interaction is vital for all children, even those with unique needs. Here are some strategies for getting your kids out and socializing:

Homeschool Groups: Get involved with local homeschooling groups that welcome children with special needs. Coops, field trips, and group activities may give valuable social experiences.

Extracurricular Activities: Enroll your kid in extracurricular activities that match their interests and talents. This might include everything from adaptive sports programs to painting courses.

Playdates and Meetups: Schedule get-togethers and playdates with other children. As your child grows used to the group, gradually increase the size from small, manageable beginning groups.

Celebrating Achievements

Achievement Boards: Create an achievement board to showcase your child's successes. Celebrate their success with stickers, awards, and photographs.

Special Treats: Recognize successes via special snacks or activities. This may be a favorite food, a day at the park, or a movie night.

Family Celebrations: Engage the whole family in celebrating achievements. It's an excellent approach to express support and make your youngster feel unique.

Document Progress: Maintain a diary or scrapbook of your child's accomplishments. This might be a great approach to reflect on how far they've come.Homeschooling a special needs kid is a unique and wonderful experience. Understanding their requirements, providing a friendly atmosphere, tailoring the curriculum, adding treatments, and developing a strong support network will enable you to give a satisfying and productive education. Remember, laughter and optimism can brighten even the worst days.

Chapter 11: Homeschooling Through Tough Times: When Life Gives You Lemons, Make Lesson Plans"

Let's be honest: even in the best-organized homeschooling families, life isn't always sunshine and rainbows. There will be moments when everything seems to go wrong at once. From family problems to personal sickness, homeschooling during difficult times might seem like attempting to juggle burning flames on a unicycle. But don't worry, crazy homeschool mother, because this chapter is all about negotiating those hard patches with grace, adaptability, and maybe even a giggle or two.

Recognizing Tough Times

Tough times can come in many forms. Here are some common challenges you might face:

Family crises: such as illness, death, or financial challenges, might disturb your homeschooling schedule.

Personal Health Issues: Illness may disrupt educational planning and activities for both parents and children.

Emotional Stress: Anxiety, depression, and other mental health conditions may impact both parents and children, making homeschooling tough.

External Disruptions: Natural catastrophes, community difficulties, or unforeseen occurrences may disrupt your homeschooling schedule.

Strategies for Homeschooling Through Tough Times

When life becomes rough, flexibility and adaptation become your greatest allies. Here are some ways to assist you manage:

Priorities: Prioritize the most essential topics and activities. It is OK to put certain things on hold for the time being. Consider it educational triage: save the mathematics and forgo the medieval history reenactment (unless it's a family favorite).

Simplify: Choose low-prep activities and materials. Educational films, audiobooks, and workbooks may save lives. Sometimes a documentary marathon is just what everyone needs.

Routine, Not Rigidity: Maintain a basic schedule to offer structure while being flexible. Some days may need to begin with a pajama day or conclude with an unexpected family movie night.

Self-Care: Prioritize self-care to better support your family. This may be taking a sleep while the kids watch an instructive program or getting in a bubble bath during "recess."

Ask for Help: Seek assistance from family, friends, or the homeschooling community.

Don't be embarrassed to ask for assistance with meals, errands, or even just a sympathetic ear.

Include the Kids: Communicate with your children in age-appropriate ways and include them in problem solving. We typically underestimate children's resilience and comprehension.

Alternative Learning Methods

During difficult circumstances, it is completely okay to think creatively and use other learning approaches. Educational television series and movies provide several great learning opportunities, converting your screen into a cinematic school. Just ready for your children to begin quoting their favorite characters.
Audiobooks and podcasts are ideal for studying on-the-go or when you're too sleepy to read aloud. They're also great for quiet time since the tales are often narrated by professional actors who bring the characters to life.
Online learning sites and programs, such as Khan Academy, Coursera, and YouTube, may help relieve some of the stress by delivering high-quality instructional material.
Hands-on activity, such as cooking, gardening, and basic scientific experiments, need little preparation and provide many learning opportunities. Educational games and puzzles make learning enjoyable and participatory, with board games teaching arithmetic, strategy, and collaboration.

Creating a Safe Space

When things go rough, it's crucial to provide a secure and comfortable environment for your family.
Make sure everyone has access to their favorite comfort objects, such as plush animals, blankets, and books.
Create a quiet space for relaxation and breaks. Fill it with cushions, soothing lighting, and relaxing hobbies such as coloring books.
Maintain a happy and encouraging atmosphere. Use positive phrases and concentrate on what is going well, no matter how minor.

Long-Term Planning

When you are going through a difficult period, it is easy to get overwhelmed. Here's how to maintain a long-term perspective.

Focus on the Big Picture: Remember that homeschooling is a long-term process, not a quick fix. Missing a few days or even weeks of scheduled study will not disrupt your child's education.

Document the Journey: Keep a diary or scrapbook of your homeschooling experience, including challenging periods. Documenting your experiences may be therapeutic and serve as a memorable souvenir for the future.

Reassess and alter: Regularly review your objectives and alter strategies as appropriate. Flexibility is essential for managing homeschooling during difficult circumstances.

Homeschooling during difficult circumstances is no easy task, but with patience, adaptability, and a sense of humor, you can overcome the obstacles and emerge stronger on the other side. Remember that it's alright to take days off and seek help when you need it. The well-being of your family comes first.

Chapter 12: Homeschooling High School: Surviving the Teen Years and Preparing for the Future

Homeschooling high school may be like conquering Mount Everest. It's difficult, requires careful preparation, and sometimes results in altitude sickness (or, in this instance, adolescent angst). But don't worry, crazy homeschool mother; with the correct methods and a decent sense of humor, you can not only survive but flourish in high school. In this chapter, we'll look at how to homeschool a teenager, from academics to preparation for college and career, while making things as enjoyable and interesting as possible.

Understanding Teenagers: Basics

First, let us admit the obvious: teens are a distinct species. They are negotiating a complicated world of hormones, identity, and independence. Here's how to maintain your sanity.

Patience is key: Patience is not just a virtue; it is a survival skill. When your adolescent rolls their eyes for the hundredth time in an hour, take a deep breath and realize that it will pass.

Maintain open communication: Teens like being heard, even if they don't always show it. Regular check-ins and honest communication may help to avoid many misunderstandings.

Respect Independence: Recognize the rising demand for independence. Give them greater flexibility over their schedules and educational options. It's remarkable how responsible kids can become when allowed some freedom (and the odd push).

Creating a High School Curriculum

High school demands a more planned and challenging curriculum. Here's how to create one that will prepare your adolescent for the future. Ensure your program includes English, Math, Science, and Social Studies. These are required for college preparation and a comprehensive education.

Select electives and topics that match your teen's interests and future ambitions. This might include anything from art and music to computer technology and culinary skills.
Consider advanced courses, such as AP or honors classes. Online platforms and local co-ops often provide these. They may give the necessary challenge for your kid while also looking fantastic on college applications.
Remember to integrate life skills such as personal budgeting, cooking, and time management. These are as vital to academic courses and will help your kid prepare for independent life.

Keeping High School Engaging

Even in high school, learning should be enjoyable and interesting. Here's how you can keep your adolescent engaged.

Use project-based learning to allow your adolescent to investigate subjects in detail. This might involve research projects, community work, or developing a business proposal. Provide real-world learning opportunities such as internships, volunteer work, or part-time employment. These chances teach kids essential skills and help them improve their resumes.
Field excursions aren't limited to younger students. Plan field trips that are relevant to your teen's academics, such as visiting a local court for a civics lesson or a tech business for a computer science class.
Use interactive technology and internet resources to enhance learning experiences. Virtual laboratories, online simulations, and instructional applications may all improve the learning experience.

Preparing for College and Career

High school is all about preparing for the next stage. Here's how to help your adolescent navigate the college and career preparation process.

College Research: Start college research early. Look for programs that align with your teen's interests and professional objectives. Make a list of possible colleges and learn about their entrance criteria.

Standardized Tests: Prepare for standardized examinations such as the SAT and ACT. Use prep materials, online courses, and practice exams. Remember that a good night's sleep and a healthy breakfast will help you do well on exam day.

College Applications: Guide your adolescent through the college application process. This involves drafting essays, collecting recommendations, and completing applications. Create deadlines to keep things on track.

Scholarships and Financial Aid: Research available scholarships and financial assistance possibilities. There are several options available to assist pay for a college education. Apply for as many as possible; every little bit counts.

Career Exploration: Encourage career exploration via work shadowing, internships, and aptitude testing. Help your child understand their own talents and interests, as well as how they relate to future vocations.

Building a Supportive Environment for Teens

Supporting a high school student extends beyond academics. Here's how to create a friendly environment:

Conduct regular mental health check-ins with your teenager. High school may be stressful, so it's crucial that students feel supported. Encourage open communication regarding their emotions and pressures.

Encourage your adolescent to engage with classmates. Join a homeschooling organization, club, or sports team. Social engagement is critical to their growth and well-being.
Encourage your teen's hobbies and interests. Whether it's playing an instrument, drawing, or computing, these pastimes may be a welcome escape from academics.
Use positive reinforcement to motivate your adolescent. Celebrate their accomplishments and provide critical comments on areas for development. "I'm proud of you" may go a long way.
Encourage your adolescent to maintain a balance between school, job, and leisure activities. Set limits on screen usage and study hours to ensure kids have time for everything essential.

Life Beyond High School

Not every road goes to college, and that's OK. Here are several alternate ways and how you might prepare for them.

Vocational Training: Some kids flourish in hands-on settings. Consider vocational training programs or apprenticeships in areas such as carpentry, culinary arts, or healthcare. These occupations may be rewarding and profitable, yet they do not need a mountain of school debt.

Gap Year: A gap year may provide valuable opportunities for personal growth, travel, and professional development. Help your adolescent design a meaningful gap year that reflects their interests and ambitions. Just make sure they have a strategy to avoid sitting on the sofa all year.

Entrepreneurship: Encourage your teen's entrepreneurial spirit. Help them create a business plan, acquire mentors, and perhaps establish a small company. It's an excellent approach to develop real-world skills and boost confidence.

Navigating high school and planning for the future is a tough but rewarding experience. You can put your children up for success while keeping your sanity by accepting their freedom, balancing academics and hobbies, and preparing for college or alternate routes.

Remember to take care of yourself, rely on your support system, and maintain a sense of humor. You're doing an incredible job, Crazy Homeschool Mama, and your efforts will pay off in ways you can't anticipate.

Chapter 13: Balancing Work and Homeschooling: The Ultimate Juggling Act

If you've ever attempted to hold a conference call while discussing the intricacies of long division, you know how difficult it can be to balance job and homeschooling duties. But don't worry, fellow crazy homeschool mother, since this chapter is full with advice, solutions, and a few chuckles to help you negotiate this difficult but wonderful balancing act.

Understanding the Challenge

Balancing employment and homeschooling has distinct obstacles.

Managing time effectively might be challenging while working two jobs.
Frequently transitioning between "work mode" and "teacher mode" may be psychologically draining.
Balancing employment and homeschooling may be challenging since both demand attention.
Feeling guilty about not giving 100% to both roles is typical but counterproductive.

Strategies for Success

Here are some strategies to help you manage the dual responsibilities of working and homeschooling:

Make a timetable: A well-planned timetable is your best buddy. Schedule precise times for work and homeschooling, and try to keep to them as much as possible. Use color-coding to keep things organized; it's like visual sanity.

Flexible Hours: If your employer permits, consider working flexible hours. Early mornings, late nights, and split hours might help you better manage job and homeschooling. Just be ready for strange hours and the occasional snooze attack.

Prioritize: Identify and prioritize your main priorities daily. It's acceptable if not everything is finished. The world will not end if you choose a large job assignment or a key homeschooling lesson over laundry.

Use Downtime Wisely: Make the most of your child's free time to study alone. Quiet time, reading sessions, and instructive movies may all give useful work opportunities. Just remember to check in on a regular basis to ensure that they have not constructed a fort out of your tax paperwork.

Delegate tasks: Assign domestic chores and teaching duties to your spouse or older children. This may help you reduce your workload while also teaching your children vital life skills. Remember that collaboration makes the dream work, or at least gets the dishes done.

Finding Balance: Tips for Different Scenarios

Whether you work from home or not, here are some strategies for combining both roles:

Working from home

Establish clear boundaries between work and homeschooling. Use visual indicators, such as a "Do Not Disturb" sign or a unique cap that indicates "Mom is working." Schedule breaks to spend time together. A short snack, a stroll around the block, or a few minutes of playing may all help people rejuvenate. Communicate openly with your job and clientele about your homeschooling status. Most people understand and will appreciate your candor.

When working outside the house

Consider arranging for trustworthy daycare or a homeschooling co-op to cover your work hours. This might be a spouse, family member, or close friend.
Consider homeschooling during the evenings or weekends. Flexibility is one of the benefits of homeschooling, so take use of it.
Prepare lesson plans and resources ahead of time to ensure caregivers have a clear understanding of the task at hand. Clear instructions may assist to ensure consistency.

Managing Distractions

Distractions are unavoidable, but they can be handled: Use timers, noise-cancelling headphones, and designated "quiet zones" to reduce distractions. A concentrated work atmosphere helps you and your kid remain on track.

Take useful breaks that include physical exercise. A brief workout or dance party might help you release pent-up energy and gain concentration.
Utilize the Pomodoro Technique (25 minutes of work followed by a 5-minute break) to improve productivity and attention. It's amazing how much you can do in a short, concentrated burst of effort.

Balancing job and homeschooling is not easy, but with the appropriate tactics, support, and a sense of humor, you can succeed. Remember, you're doing an excellent job managing all of your duties, and it's OK to tackle things one day at a time.

Chapter 14: Balancing Life and Homeschooling: The Ultimate Tightrope Walk

Balancing job, life, and homeschooling may seem like a high-wire performance in a three-ring circus. It's a delicate balance of prioritizing, multitasking, and sometimes just winging it. But don't worry, crazy homeschool mother, because this chapter is filled with fresh methods to help you maintain that delicate balance while keeping your sanity intact.

Mastering Multitasking

When you're homeschooling, working, and maintaining a family, multitasking is an art form. Here's how to do it successfully:

Task batching: Group comparable jobs together and complete them in committed time slots. Set out particular hours for tasks such as responding to emails, making phone calls, and arranging lessons. This reduces the mental transition needed and increases efficiency.

Integrate Learning and Chores: Combine home tasks with educational activities. Count with smaller children while sorting clothes, or make cooking a math lesson by measuring ingredients. Who knew cleaning the bathroom could be a chemical experiment?

Workstation Rotation: Set up various workstations around the home to facilitate transitions between tasks. A portable workstation, complete with a laptop and needed supplies, may be moved from the kitchen table to the living room, keeping you close to both work and your children.

Setting Realistic Goals

Setting realistic objectives for yourself and your family is critical to finding balance. Here's how to manage expectations:

Identify top three daily priorities for job, homeschooling, and domestic activities. Focus on these first, and realize that not everything will be completed. Some days, just surviving and keeping everyone fed and happy is a tremendous accomplishment.
Use flexible planning tools, such as dry-erase boards or digital planners, to allow for revisions. Plans change, children become ill, and sometimes life just happens. Embrace flexibility as a strength, not a problem.
Celebrate tiny accomplishments. Did you finish the report and the math lesson? High five! These modest celebrations boost morale and remind you that progress is being done.

Leveraging Technology

Technology may be a valuable tool for juggling work, life, and homeschooling. Here's how to use it effectively:

Use educational applications and tools to entertain your children while you concentrate on work. Apps such as Khan Academy, Duolingo, and ABC mouse may help you learn while also freeing up some time. Save time with online food shopping and delivery services. It is a game changer for busy parents. It also minimizes the likelihood of impulsive purchases - no more buying three different flavors of ice cream because you were hungry.
Join virtual homeschool co-ops and online courses. These may provide organized schooling and social contact to your children while you work. It's also an excellent method to network with other homeschooling families.

Creating Boundaries

Creating clear boundaries between work, homeschooling, and personal time is essential. Here's how to set and maintain them:

Dedicated Work Hours: Establish designated work hours and discuss them with your family. Use visual clues, such as a closed door or a "Do Not Disturb" sign, to indicate that you are in work mode even if work is your free time (you are not working mom). It helps to reduce disruptions and keep everyone on the same page.

Homeschool Hours: Set defined hours for homeschooling. Having a set start and finish time helps to establish a habit and avoids academics from taking over the whole day.

Personal Time: Make personal time a priority. Personal time, whether it's reading, exercising, or just relaxing with a cup of coffee, is essential for recharging.

Managing Stress

Balancing several responsibilities may be challenging. Here are some stress-management and well-being strategies:

Mindfulness Practices: Integrate mindfulness techniques such as meditation, deep breathing, and yoga into your everyday routine. Even a few minutes of mindfulness may greatly lessen stress.

Comedy and laughter: Don't underestimate the impact of comedy. Laughter may be an effective stress relief. Watch a hilarious program, read a witty book, or just exchange jokes with your family. Remember: laughing is the greatest medicine.

Connect with Nature: Spend time outside to recharge. A stroll in the park, gardening, or just relaxing on the porch may all help to relax and reset the mind.

Delegating and Outsourcing

You don't have to accomplish everything alone. Here's how to successfully delegate and outsource:

Consider hiring someone to assist with domestic duties. A cleaning service or part-time babysitter may help you save time and focus on more vital duties.

Involve your family in domestic tasks. Assign age-appropriate duties to your children and promote collaboration. It teaches children essential life skills while reducing your burden.

Share work with your companion. Discuss and allocate duties according to strengths and availability. Teamwork and communication are essential for managing a busy family.

Balancing job, life, and homeschooling is a tightrope walk, but with the correct tactics and a good dose of humor, all three can be managed successfully. Remember to set attainable objectives, use technology, establish clear limits, manage stress, and engage your family in the process. Also, constantly enjoy the tiny victories along the road.

Chapter 15: Finding Your Tribe: Building a Homeschooling Community

Homeschooling might often seem like a solitary effort, but it does not have to be. Establishing a homeschooling community is critical for support, socializing, and sharing resources. Finding your tribe entails surrounding yourself with individuals who understand your path and can provide company, guidance, and perhaps a few laughs along the road. In this chapter, we'll look at how to discover and establish your homeschooling community, so that both you and your children flourish.

Why a Homeschooling Community Matters

Support: Homeschool parents may provide moral support, counsel, and encouragement. It is good to know you are not alone on this road.

Socialization: Regular connection with other children and families promotes social development and a feeling of belonging.

Resource Sharing: Sharing educational materials, curricular ideas, and teaching suggestions improves homeschooling efficiency and effectiveness.

Shared Experiences: Celebrating accomplishments and facing problems together enhances the homeschooling experience.

Finding Your Homeschool Tribe

How to Find and Connect with Other Homeschoolers: Search for local homeschool organizations in your region. These clubs often plan field excursions, co-op programs, and social events. Websites like Meetup and Facebook are excellent places to start.

Participate in online communities, including forums, social media groups, and homeschooling websites. These networks provide a wealth of knowledge and the opportunity to interact with homeschoolers from all around the globe.

Just be prepared for a lot of acronyms; TWTM, CM, and others will become second nature rather fast.

Local community centers and libraries offer homeschooling programs and activities. Check with them. Many provide programs, organizations, and activities designed exclusively for homeschooling families.

Attend Homeschooling Conferences and Conventions. These events are great for meeting other homeschoolers, attending seminars, and discovering new resources. In addition, there is generally a vendor area filled with tantalizing instructional items.

Enroll your children in extracurricular activities such as athletics, music, art, and scouting. These events provide social contact and the opportunity to meet other homeschooling families who have similar interests.

Building and Nurturing Your Community

Once you've identified your tribe, here's how to cultivate those relationships:

Organize Regular Meetups: Schedule frequent gatherings for playdates, field excursions, and co-op programs. Consistent engagement promotes solid bonds between children and parents. And, let's be honest, it's great to have another adult to talk to while the children play.

Create Study Groups: Form study groups for tough topics, such as scientific projects or literary debates. It's incredible how much more fascinating a Shakespeare play can be when performed with friends.

Collaborate: Share teaching duties with other parents. If one parent excels in math while the other excels at art, switch classes to provide a well-rounded education for all children. It also allows you to take a vacation from things that you are less enthused about.

Support each other: Offer and receive help during difficult times. Mutual assistance enriches the community, whether it is by lending a listening ear, assisting with teaching, or trading babysitting tasks.

Celebrate Together: Celebrate milestones and successes with the group. Organize graduation ceremonies, scientific fairs, and art displays. These activities promote a feeling of achievement and communal pride.

Tips for Effective Community Building

Effective community development involves work and a good attitude. Here are some suggestions to bear in mind:

Be inclusive: Accept families from all origins and homeschooling views. A varied community enhances the learning experience for everybody.

Communicate openly: and honestly with your community members.

Clear communication minimizes misunderstandings and ensures that everyone's demands are addressed.

Stay Organized: Use online calendars, group chats, and email lists to keep everyone updated on forthcoming events and activities. Organization keeps things running smoothly and guarantees that no one misses out.

Be flexible: Recognize that not every family will be able to participate in all activities. Be adaptable and accommodating to various schedules and responsibilities.

Show appreciation: Recognize and value the efforts of community members. A simple thank you may go a long way towards sustaining great connections.

The Power of Collaboration

Collaboration within your homeschooling group may result in extraordinary experiences. Here's how to maximize collaboration opportunities:

Joint Projects: Plan cooperative initiatives that bring together various families. This may be a communal garden, a joint art project, or a scientific fair. Joint initiatives promote collaboration and a feeling of achievement.

Guest Speakers: Invite guest speakers from the community to share their skills. Parents with unique abilities or professional backgrounds may provide useful lessons and insights.

Resource Pooling: Combine resources for costly or seldom utilized commodities. Share instructional resources, scientific equipment, and even textbooks. This strategy makes homeschooling more cost-effective and resource-rich.

Team Learning: Utilize team-based learning strategies for topics that benefit from group engagement. Group discussions, cooperative learning exercises, and team challenges may help make learning more dynamic and interesting.

Building Lifelong Friendships

Finding your homeschool tribe may lead to lifetime connections, which is one of the most enjoyable elements of the experience. Here's how to foster these relationships:

Plan family trips that extend beyond homeschooling activities. Picnics, hiking vacations, and game evenings all assist to strengthen family bonds.

Create a support network for both children and parents. Regular check-ins, encouraging texts, and being there for one another during difficult times deepen these ties.

Celebrate holidays and special events together. Holiday parties, birthday celebrations, and seasonal activities foster long-lasting memories and traditions.

Encourage peer support by having older children mentor younger ones. Peer support encourages children to take responsibility and develop strong, supportive connections.

Creating a homeschooling community is an important component of the homeschooling process. By establishing your tribe, cultivating connections, and partnering on educational and social activities, you can provide a rich, supportive environment for your family. Remember that a vibrant community not only improves the educational experience, but also gives a network of friends who understand and support your individual path.

Chapter 16: Dad's Role: Tag-Teaming the Teaching

Sure, the book is subtitled "Crazy Homeschool Mama," but let's be honest: both parents can (and should) participate in the homeschooling journey. There's plenty of opportunity for everyone to engage in the fun, whether Dad is taking the teaching reins while Mom conquers the corporate jungle or both parents are teaming up for the homeschool day. So, let's speak about how fathers may play an important (and often humorous) part in the homeschooling experience.

The Dynamic Duo: Sharing the Load

In the homeschooling world, sharing tasks may transform parents into the ultimate dynamic pair. Here's how to make tag-team teaching both productive and enjoyable:

Divide and Conquer: Identify each other's abilities and assign tasks appropriately. Allow Dad and Mom to take the lead in their areas of competence, such as arithmetic and history. This allows each parent to shine, while the children benefit from a variety of teaching styles.

Scheduling Swaps: For parents juggling work and homeschooling, establish a flexible calendar to ensure seamless transitions. Maybe Dad handles the morning math marathons while Mom manages the afternoon painting sessions. Think of it as the ultimate relay race, but without the uncomfortable baton handoff.

Collaborative Planning: Collaboratively develop the curriculum and daily routine. This ensures that both parents understand and support each other. Furthermore, planning meetings provide you excellent opportunity to get takeout and discuss over a platter of nachos.

Dad's Unique Teaching Style

Dads often provide a distinct touch to homeschooling, which may be likened to combining stand-up comedy with academics. Here's how to appreciate Dad's unique teaching style:

Dads generally excel at hands-on learning. Whether he's constructing a birdhouse, performing backyard scientific experiments, or transforming the living room into a Lego engineering lab,

Dad's ability for hands-on learning is vital. Just have a mop available in case those "experiments" go dirty.

Dads excel at making learning enjoyable. They may convert a tedious grammar drill into a fun game, or a history lecture into a grand narrative event. Remember that dramatic voices and spontaneous reenactments are the most effective ways to teach the Gettysburg Address.

Dad can turn every excursion into an educational experience. Dads excel at turning regular days into epic journeys for information, whether it's trekking through nature trails or touring local museums. And if you get lost, consider it an impromptu geography lesson.

The Power of Dad Jokes

Never underestimate the educational value of a good dad joke. Here's how to use the power of comedy in homeschooling:

Use classic dad jokes to add fun to arithmetic lectures. "Why did the equal symbol seem so humble? Because he was neither less nor greater than everyone else. Sure, the youngsters may sigh, but they will certainly remember the lesson!

Use puns and jokes to make history more entertaining. "Why did the scarecrow become an effective teacher?

Because he excelled in his specialty!" You'd be astonished at how much historical information stays when provided with a joke.

Use comedy to explain complicated scientific subjects. "What is the term for an educated tube?" "A graduated cylinder." Corny? Absolutely. However, it's an excellent way to brighten the atmosphere and make studying more pleasurable.

The Benefits of Dad's Involvement

Dad's active involvement in homeschooling provides several advantages. Here's what makes it a game changer:

Role Modeling: Dads who educate their children provide a positive example of lifelong learning and work ethic. Seeing Dad tackle a difficult job or delve into a new topic teaches children that learning never ends, and neither does the devotion to education.

Diverse Perspectives: Dad's unique viewpoint helps the learning process. Diverse origins, interests, and teaching methods provide a well-rounded education and keep things interesting. It's like having a smorgasbord of educational options to choose from every day.

Stronger Family Bonds: Sharing the homeschooling experience promotes family relationships. Working together to solve issues, celebrate victories, and overcome hurdles fosters a strong feeling of camaraderie and unity.

Plus, there's something special about celebrating the accomplishment of finally unraveling the puzzle of long-standing separation as a family.

Dads offer their own brand of enchantment to homeschooling, whether via hands-on learning, comedy, or just serving as an adventure guide on the educational trip. By sharing teaching duties, both parents may contribute to a rich, varied, and interesting homeschool experience.

Chapter 17: Math Mayhem: How to Teach Math at All Levels (Without Losing Your Mind)

The subject that brings equal parts excitement and dread. From counting apples in kindergarten to solving quadratic equations in high school, math is a journey that evolves with your child's age and abilities. As a Crazy Homeschool Mama, you'll need to navigate this wild terrain with creativity, patience, and a sense of humor. Buckle up, because we're about to embark on the rollercoaster of teaching math through different school stages.

Teaching Math: The Universal Struggle

Let's face it: teaching math at any level may be a common challenge. Here's how to tackle math with comedy and creativity at every stage:

Allow for occasional math meltdowns. You're attempting to explain long division, and your youngster looks at you as if you've sprouted a second head. Take a big breath, chuckle, and try again tomorrow.

Calculators have a habit of vanishing just when you need them. Embrace the quest and make it a game. "Whoever finds the calculator gets to choose tonight's dessert!"

Use arithmetic jokes to lighten the atmosphere. "Why was six afraid of seven?" Because seven, eight (ate) nine!" Groans are sure, as are smiles.

Using hands-on activities may be effective in teaching arithmetic. From making cookies to constructing birdhouses, take advantage of every opportunity to teach arithmetic. Your youngster will be so engrossed that they won't know they're learning.

Use a timer to motivate your youngster to complete tasks. "Let's see how many problems you can solve in five minutes!" It provides a feeling of urgency and enjoyment to the endeavor.

Surviving the Frustration

The math can be frustrating. Here's how to keep your cool when things get tough:

Take a break when you or your kid get irritated. Step away from the arithmetic problems and do something enjoyable for a while. Sometimes all you need is a brief getaway to return with a new perspective.

Keep your sense of humor. Laugh at the errors and bewilderment. It's only arithmetic; it isn't worth losing your mind over. Remember that even mathematicians had to study math at some time.

Don't be scared to ask for assistance. Whether it's using an online resource, a tutor, or a buddy who enjoys math, gaining a new viewpoint may make all the difference.

Celebrating the Wins

When your child finally gets it, celebrate! Here's how to make those math victories even sweeter:

Plan a math-themed celebration. Have food in shapes (such as pizza pieces or pie), play arithmetic games, and award "math magician" certificates. It's a fun method to reinforce what they've learned and recognize their hard effort.

Create a brag board to share math accomplishments. It serves as a visible reminder of their progress and a powerful incentive for future classes.

Implement a reward system to encourage mastery of arithmetic topics. Stickers, increased screen time, or a little toy may provide excellent rewards.

Kindergarten: Counting on Fun

Welcome to the realm of numbers! Kindergarten math is all about exposing your kid to fundamental concepts in an enjoyable and engaging manner.

Convert everyday activities into counting games. Count the steps to the park, pieces of fruit for snack time, and toys to clean up. "One, two, three... okay, now let's see how many socks we can find under the couch!"

Use melodies and rhymes to make numbers memorable. "One, two, buckle my shoe" is a classic, but feel free to be creative and write your own songs. Bonus points if you can maintain a straight face while singing.

Teach fundamental addition and subtraction using toys such as blocks and LEGOs. "If we have five red blocks and take away two, how many are left?" It combines math with fun.

Elementary School: The Building Blocks

As your kid moves through primary school, arithmetic gets more regimented, but it may still be enjoyable.

Incorporate math-themed board and card games. "Monopoly" teaches money management, "Uno" aids with number identification, and even "War" may reinforce greater than/less than ideas.

Use real-life experiences to teach arithmetic. Cooking is fantastic for fractions and measures, while shopping excursions may aid with addition, subtraction, and even percentages during a bargain.

Use visual aids such as charts, graphs, and manipulatives to clarify complex ideas. Multiplication tables, vivid charts, and interactive applications may make math lessons more enjoyable.

Middle School: The Plot Thickens

With the addition of algebra, geometry, and other topics, middle school math becomes increasingly challenging. It is a pivotal stage in which abstract thinking takes center stage.

Utilize internet resources, apps, and videos to enhance your teaching. Websites such as Khan Academy provide interactive courses that may help people understand tough subjects.

Engage students in math challenges and contests to make learning fun. Set up timed quizzes, math scavenger hunts, or friendly contests with other homeschooling families.

Demonstrate real-world math applications. Math abilities may be used in practical ways like budgeting for a project, calculating distances on a map, or constructing a basic garden layout.

High School: The Final Frontier

Trigonometry, calculus, and advanced algebra are all examples of difficult high school math topics. However, with the appropriate attitude, you can assist your kid in navigating these tricky seas.

Encourage your adolescent to be self-directed in their learning. Use a range of materials, such as textbooks, online courses, and tutoring as needed. This is also an excellent opportunity to expose them to study groups or math clubs.

Integrate mathematics into broader endeavors. Building a model, carrying out a scientific experiment, or evaluating data for a research article might all need sophisticated math abilities.

Prepare your adolescent for standardized examinations like the SAT or ACT. Practice examinations, preparation courses, and study books may make a significant impact. It's also a wonderful approach to refresh your memory on long-forgotten formulae.

Teaching arithmetic at any level does not have to be a misery. With imagination, patience, and a decent sense of humor, you can make arithmetic enjoyable and clear for your youngster. Remember that you are not alone in this; even the finest instructors struggled with arithmetic at some time.

Chapter 18: Science Experiments: When the Kitchen Turns into a Lab

Alright, Crazy Homeschool Mama, it's time to put on your lab coat (or at least an old T-shirt) and explore the amazing world of scientific projects. Homeschool science involves more than simply reading textbooks and memorizing the periodic table. It's about getting your hands filthy, creating a mess, and sometimes causing a little explosion. And what better place to accomplish this than in the heart of the home: the kitchen? Prepare for a crazy adventure as we transform your kitchen into a laboratory!

The Kitchen Lab Setup

First and foremost, prepare your kitchen for its makeover into a research lab. Here is how to start:

Designate a space: Clear a part of your kitchen counter or table. This will be your official laboratory area. Make sure it is far enough away from the stove and any open flames (we are here for safe science, not accidental fireworks).

Stock up on supplies: Gather basic ingredients such as baking soda, vinegar, food coloring, cornstarch, and dish soap. These common substances may be used in a variety of experiments. Don't forget your safety goggles; nothing screams "serious scientist" like huge goggles.

Protective gear: Aprons, gloves, and old T-shirts will be useful for you and your mini-scientists. This is not just for safety; it is also an excellent method to prevent permanently tie-dying your beloved garments with food coloring.

Organize your tools: Keep measuring cups, spoons, mixing bowls, and pipettes (or plastic droppers) nearby. Label everything clearly. You don't want to confuse sugar for salt unless you want to have a surprising response.

Classic Kitchen Experiments

Now that your kitchen lab is complete, let's get started with some classic scientific experiments that are sure to wow your kids while also teaching them something.

The Baking Soda and Vinegar Volcano: A classic scientific experiment. Combine baking soda and vinegar and see the foamy eruption. Add some red food coloring to enhance the "lava" appearance. It's like having a little, non-lethal Mount Vesuvius on your kitchen counter.

Oobleck: Make oobleck by combining cornstarch and water, resulting in a non-Newtonian fluid that may be both liquid and solid. It's an excellent approach to expose children to the marvels of physics. Furthermore, it's constantly fascinating to poke, prod, and attempt to punch without spraying anything.

Dancing Raisins: To make Dancing Raisins, pour clear soda into a glass and add raisins. Watch them dance up and down in the bubbles.

This easy experiment is an excellent method to demonstrate buoyancy and gas release. It's like a dried fruit rave party.

Homemade Lava Lamp: Create a homemade lava lamp by filling a glass jar with water, adding food coloring, and topping it with vegetable oil. Drop in an Alka-Seltzer tablet and watch as colorful water blobs rise and fall. It's fascinating and an excellent introduction to density and chemical reactions.

The Great Mess Management

Science experiments are enjoyable, but they are often untidy. Here's how to handle pandemonium without losing your cool:

Use old newspapers, plastic tablecloths, or huge trays to catch spills and splashes. This manner, your kitchen will not resemble a murder scene after each experiment.

Make cleanup part of the experiment. Assign jobs to your children: one sweeps the table, another rinses the bowls. It's an excellent technique to instill responsibility and collaboration. Furthermore, numerous hands make light labor (with less sticky floors).

Prepare for things to go wrong. The vinegar may leak, the food coloring may tip over, or the baking soda may erupt more vigorously than anticipated. Laugh it off and use it as a teaching moment: "Well, kids, that's what we call an unexpected variable!"

Turning Mistakes into Learning Opportunities

Science is all about experimenting, so things don't always go as planned. Accept your errors and utilize them as learning moments:

The Exploding Bag: Did making a sandwich bag rocket result in vinegar all over the ceiling? Not an issue. Discuss what went wrong and how to improve the experiment next time. Perhaps invest on a step ladder and some nice ceiling cleanser.

The Failed Slime: Slime may not always work as intended. Maybe you used too much borax or not enough adhesive. Instead of throwing it away, try other ratios to find what works. Remember, Edison didn't fail 1,000 times; he discovered 1,000 methods not to manufacture a lightbulb.

The Color Run: Did you mix food coloring and end up with rainbow-colored hands? This is an excellent time to discuss why food coloring stains and how to remove them. Furthermore, colorful hands make for a terrific narrative and some intriguing stares in the grocery shop.

Keeping Your Sanity

Managing a culinary lab might be intimidating, but here are some strategies to help you stay sane:

Plan ahead: Gather all necessary items before beginning.

Nothing is worse than learning you've run out of vinegar halfway through an experiment. A little planning may go a long way.

Set Clear Rules: Set clear guidelines for your kitchen lab. No eating the experiments (unless they're safe and tasty), no running with scissors, and always clean up after yourself.

Enjoy the process: Remember: the objective is to make science enjoyable and interesting. Enjoy the process, no matter how dirty or crazy it is. Your excitement will be infectious.

Using your kitchen as a lab is one of the most enjoyable and informative components of homeschooling. Accept the chaos, laugh at your missteps, and savor the amazing moments of discovery. You're not simply teaching science; you're making memories and instilling a passion of learning.

So, Crazy Homeschool Mama, put on your lab coat, mix up some baking soda and vinegar, and enter into the realm of culinary science with excitement. You have got this!

Chapter 19: History Lessons: Making the Past Less Boring

History is a topic that sometimes elicits moans and eye rolls from children who don't understand why they have to study about "old stuff." But, as a Crazy Homeschool Mama, you understand that history is more than just dates and names; it is the story of humanity, full of drama, intrigue, and lessons that are still relevant today. So, how can you make history classes interesting and enjoyable? Buckle up, because we are going to turn your homeschool history lessons into a thrilling voyage through time.

The Power of Storytelling

History is essentially a collection of tales. Embrace the story element to make it more interesting:

Be a Storyteller: Transform historical occurrences into tales. Make use of dramatic voices, sound effects, and descriptive descriptions to bring events to life. "Once upon a time, in a land far, far away called Ancient Egypt, a young pharaoh named Tutankhamun ruled with wisdom and curiosity..."

Make cliffhangers: Like a good TV program, conclude your history lectures on a cliffhanger. "Just when everyone believed the conflict was done, something entirely unexpected occurred.

But we will find out what it was tomorrow!" This keeps your children excited to see what occurs next.

Historical characters: Concentrate on the individuals behind the events. Instead of dry data, describe the tales of historical characters, including their goals, hardships, and accomplishments. How did Cleopatra enchant Julius Caesar? What made Joan of Arc so fearless? Personal tales make history more accessible and memorable.

Hands-On History

Engage your children in activities that bring history to life.

Dressing the Part: Costumes can bring history to life. Plan a "History Dress-Up Day" in which you and your children dress as historical characters. Costumes, such as togas for ancient Rome or bonnets for pioneer days, give a fun, physical aspect to learning.

Reenactments: Perform mini-reenactments of historical events. Create basic scripts and have your children act out situations. This not only reinforces what students have already learned, but it also makes the lesson more participatory and memorable. It's also an excellent method to sneak in some theater practice.

Crafts and Projects: Incorporate crafts and projects related to historical lectures. Make a model of a medieval fortress, Egyptian jewels, or Native American headdresses. Hands-on projects serve to reinforce information and make learning enjoyable.

Incorporating Technology

Explore the past with current technology, including virtual field visits to museums, historical locations, and reenactments. Many institutions provide online tours, allowing you to study artifacts and exhibitions from the comfort of your own home. It's like being transported across time without leaving your living room.

Various online games and applications may educate history. These may convert studying into a game, allowing your children to construct ancient civilizations, travel through historical events, and solve riddles about historical times.

To learn about history, watch documentaries and historically correct movies. Discuss what you've seen and compare it to what you've learnt. It's an excellent approach to witness history in action and identify any "Hollywood-ized" errors.

Making Connections

Help your children understand the significance of history in today's world.

Current Events: Link historical events to modern occurrences. Discuss how history has impacted the current world and how knowing the past may help us navigate the present. "Remember how the Great Depression prompted reforms in economic policies? Let's see how today's economic difficulties are addressed similarly or differently."

Family History: Explore your family's history. Investigate your lineage and explain how your family fits into larger historical settings. "Great-grandpa participated in World War II. Let's study more about the war and how it affected him."

Cultural History: Research the history of many cultures and civilizations. This promotes a greater awareness and respect for the world's variety. Try making traditional foods, listening to music, and learning about traditions from the eras and locations you study.

Keeping it Light and Fun

To keep your children interested in history studies, use comedy and enjoyment.

Use historical memes and jokes to improve the atmosphere. There is a whole universe of instructional comedy out there that may help you appreciate your classes more. "Why did the scarecrow become an accomplished historian? Because he excelled in his specialty!"

Encourage your youngsters to maintain a "time travel diary." They may write diary entries as if they were living throughout the historical eras you're researching. "Dear Diary, today I helped my family pick grains in ancient Egypt. "It was hot, but I enjoyed riding the Nile River with my friends."

Prepare dishes from various historical periods. Try medieval stews, antique Roman bread, and pioneer pancakes.

It's an enjoyable approach to learn about history and connect with the past. Furthermore, it's an excuse to consume something delicious in the name of knowledge.

Overcoming Challenges

History may be a difficult topic to teach, but here are some strategies to help you overcome typical challenges:

Dealing with Dry Material: Not all historical themes are engaging. When dealing with dull content, look for amusing stories or lesser-known facts that may pique your attention. Did you know George Washington enjoyed ice cream? Or was Napoleon terrified of cats?

Dealing with Difficult and Sensitive Topics: History encompasses challenging and sensitive topics. Approach these issues with caution and age-appropriate explanations. Use these chances to teach empathy, critical thinking, and the value of learning from the past.

Keeping Attention: If your children are losing interest, try several strategies to keep their attention. Incorporate a variety of activities, take pauses, and always be prepared to adjust. Remember that flexibility is one of the most valuable aspects of homeschooling.

History does not need to be dull. History lessons may be made interesting and exciting for your children by including narrative, hands-on activities, technology, and current events. Take use of the creativity and freedom that homeschooling provides, and transform history into a time travel experience.

So, Crazy Homeschool Mama, take your imagined time machine and prepare to discover the amazing realm of history. With a little zeal and a lot of creativity, you can bring the past to life for your children.

Chapter 20:
Art Class: Crafting Chaos

Art class is a great opportunity for your children to express themselves, acquire new skills, and create a beautiful mess in the process. So grab your smocks and join us in the creating frenzy!

The Setup: Preparing for the Mayhem

First things first, you must prepare your creative studio. And by "art space," I mean the whole home, since we all know that art projects have a tendency to go beyond their intended boundaries.

The Art Cart: Invest in a movable art cart to store all materials. Fill it with crayons, markers, colored pencils, paint, brushes, scissors, and enough glue sticks to construct a life-size copy of the Eiffel Tower. You could want to call it "Mom's Sanity Saver" since having everything in one location can help you avoid numerous meltdowns.

Plastic Sheeting: Use plastic sheeting to protect your flooring and furnishings. Your kitchen table will thank you, and you may escape the unpleasant topic of why there is a permanent blue stain on the hardwood floors. Think of it as an insurance policy against innovation.

Old Clothes: Label outdated garments as "art outfits." These are the garments that you don't mind being splattered with paint, glue, or glitter. loads and loads of glitter. Think of it as their artist outfit, but without the beret.

Organized Chaos: Developed a way to organize finished artwork, reducing chaos. Invest in some inexpensive frames, a clothesline with clothespins, or a large corkboard. It's an excellent method to exhibit their work while also preventing the fridge from becoming an impenetrable wall of finger drawings.

The First Project: Diving In

Starting with a basic activity, such as painting, is an excellent approach to interest your children.

It's easy, enjoyable, and certain to yield some masterpieces - or at least some intriguing splatters.

Paint Explosion: Did you squeeze too hard on the paint bottle? Congratulations, you have just completed your first abstract masterpiece on the kitchen wall. This is why we use plastic sheeting, guys. Also, have some wet wipes on hand; you'll need them more than you think.

Brush Wars: Expect sibling squabbles over "good" brushes. Keep a few spares on hand to prevent a full-fledged brush fight. Better still, let them paint with sponges, fingers, or even cotton swabs. Variety is the spice of life, and it minimizes the chances of someone getting a paintbrush in their eye.

Masterpieces in the Making: Display your children's artwork on the fridge, walls, or ceiling to save room. Don't worry if it looks more like a Rorschach test than a Monet; it's the process that matters. Set up a "Art Gallery" in a corridor or a unique section of the room to make them feel like true artists.

Sculpture Time: 3D Adventures

Ready to step it up a notch? Let's make some three-dimensional art using clay, playdough, and whatever else you can form into shapes.

Clay Catastrophes: Clay can go everywhere, including hair, nails, and dog fur. Keep some wet wipes on hand and be prepared to clean up after bath time.

Remember, the more messes they make, the more fun they have.

Playdough Parties: Playdough parties: Homemade playdough is simple to create and a huge success. Just be prepared for the eventual color combination. That amazing rainbow set you created?

It is now a murky brown glob. But hey, it's a unique brown glob! Encourage them to design certain themes or personalities to help keep the clutter under control.

Recycled Sculptures: Create recycled sculptures using items from the recycling bin. Cardboard boxes, paper towel rolls, and plastic bottles may be transformed into robots, castles, or spacecraft. You're also educating the kids about recycling, so you're doing two things at once. Challenge them to create something utilitarian, such as a pencil holder or a bird feeder.

The Great Glitter Debate

Glitter. It's the craft world's version of herpes: once it's there, it's there to stay. But it's also dazzling and entertaining, and kids like it. So, how can you handle glitter without losing your mind?

Containment: To confine the glitter explosion, use a shallow box or tray. This manner, at least portion of the glitter remains in one location. (Some. Not all. Let's be realistic here. You might even set up a "glitter station" that is only permitted in a certain location.

Glitter Glue: Consider using glitter glue instead of loose glitter, which may be overwhelming. It's less messy while yet providing the glitter that youngsters want. Furthermore, it is more difficult to spill a full bottle of glitter glue than a shaker of loose glitter. It strikes the ideal balance between glitter and sanity.

Vacuum Ready: Keep a vacuum or portable vacuum handy. You will need it. Frequently. Perhaps invest on one exclusively for your painting studio. Consider it an important homeschooling resource. Don't be shocked if you still discover glitter in unexpected locations months later.

The Art of Clean-Up

Clean-up is an essential step in the process, and it may be as chaotic as the production phase. Here's how to manage it without a tantrum.

Art Clean-Up Songs: Make a playlist of entertaining, cheerful tunes for cleanup time. Music improves everything, and it can transform the dreaded clean-up into a tiny dance party. "Clean up, clean up, everybody everywhere..." You could find yourself singing along.

Divide and conquer: Assign cleaning responsibilities to each youngster. One person cleans the table, another sweeps the floor, and another rinses the brushes.
It demonstrates collaboration while also teaching accountability. Plus, it's much easier than doing everything yourself.

Reward the Effort: Create a reward system to recognize hard work. Perhaps it's an additional tale at bedtime, a tiny treat, or just a huge embrace and plenty of praise. Positive reinforcement does wonders. Also, remember to reward yourself with a well-deserved break.

Celebrating the Creativity

Celebrate your children's inventiveness and enjoyment of producing art:

Art Shows: Organize a tiny art display at home. Display the artwork, invite family members (virtually if required), and make your children proud of their accomplishments. Make it a special occasion by serving nice appetizers. It's an excellent method to build their confidence and demonstrate their hard work.

Art Awards: Create fun art awards such as "Best Use of Glitter," "Most Colorful," and "Most Abstract." It is a great approach to recognize their efforts and inventiveness. And who doesn't like earning a little acknowledgment for their efforts?

Art Journals: Encourage youngsters to maintain art notebooks to record their favorite works, notes, and tales about their creations. It's a beautiful souvenir and an excellent method to document their creative development. It's also an excellent method to keep all of your works together.

Art Swaps: Organize art swaps with other homeschooling families. It's an excellent method for children to learn about diverse styles and approaches while also feeling like they're part of a wider creative community. Furthermore, it's a wonderful opportunity to network with other homeschooling families and exchange ideas.

Beyond the Basics

Once you've mastered the fundamentals, consider branching out into more complicated tasks.

Themed Art Days: Organize themed art days to concentrate on a certain style, artist, or medium. One day may be dedicated to Picasso and abstract art, while another to Van Gogh and impressionism. It's a wonderful method to try out new styles and approaches.

Art History Lessons: Incorporate art history into your teachings. Learn about notable painters, their methods, and the historical background for their work. It's an excellent approach to mix history and art in a fun and interesting manner.

Art Challenges: Set up art challenges for your children. Give them a prompt or a theme to see what they can come up with. It's an excellent approach to foster creativity and think beyond the box.

Art class in a homeschool context is a wonderful, messy, and chaotic experience. It's about more than simply making things; it's about expressing yourself, experimenting, and having fun with the process.

Chapter 21:
Physical Education: Turning Chores into Gym Class

Physical education is often associated with dodgeball, jump ropes, and embarrassing times in gym class. However, as a Crazy Homeschool Mama, you have the ability to reinvent physical education by skillfully incorporating it into your everyday routine. Why not turn those tedious duties into a workout? With a little imagination and humor, you can get your kids moving and grooving while maintaining your home in tip-top condition. Let's explore the crazy world of chore-based physical education!

The Importance of Physical Education for Kids of All Ages

Before we get into the details, let's discuss why physical education is so important for children at all stages of development. Understanding its advantages will make our PE choreography lessons much more effective.

Preschoolers:
Building the Foundation

Physical exercise is essential for toddlers because it helps them develop fundamental motor skills, coordination, and balance. It's also an important moment for children to understand their bodies and how they move.

Motor Skills: Activities like running, leaping, and throwing improve gross motor abilities. Fine motor abilities are acquired by doing activities such as picking up tiny items and handling equipment.

Coordination and Balance: Simple games and exercises enhance coordination and balance, laying the groundwork for more advanced physical pursuits later on.

Social Skills: Preschoolers learn social skills via group activities, like taking turns, sharing, and playing together.

Elementary School Kids: Strengthening and Learning

As children grow, physical education helps them develop strength, endurance, and flexibility. It is also an important time for children to learn about the benefits of physical exercise and good habits.

Strength and Endurance: PE exercises improve muscular strength and cardiovascular endurance, supporting overall health and fitness.

Flexibility: Stretching and range-of-motion exercises enhance flexibility, lowering the risk of injury.

Healthy Habits: Encouraging children to engage in physical exercise promotes long-term healthy behaviors.

Middle Schoolers: Navigating Changes

Middle school is a period of fast development and change. Physical education allows students to channel their energy and handle the physical and mental hurdles of puberty.

Physical Growth: Regular exercise may assist manage puberty's fast physical development and changes.

Mental Health: Physical exercise improves mental health by reducing stress, anxiety, and mood swings. It improves self-esteem and body image.

Social Connections: Middle schoolers benefit from team sports and group activities, which promote social relationships and collaboration.

High Schoolers: Preparing for the Future

For high school students, physical education is about staying healthy, planning for the future, and juggling the responsibilities of school, employment, and social life.

Fitness Maintenance: Regular exercise helps high school students maintain a healthy weight, develop muscle, and strengthen their hearts.

Life Skills: Physical education instills valuable life skills such as time management, discipline, and tenacity.

Future Preparation: PE prepares high school students for collegiate athletics, recreational sports, and remaining active by helping them develop and accomplish fitness objectives.

Preparing for the PE-Chore-Olympics

To make your home into a PE paradise, you must first set the scene. Here is how to prepare.

The Uniform: Dress professionally. Get everyone into comfortable exercise gear. Bonus points for matching headbands and wristbands, which add to the official gym class atmosphere. Remember to warm up with some gentle stretches; you don't want anybody hurting a muscle while vacuuming.

The Equipment: Organize your "gym" equipment. Brooms, mops, dusters, laundry baskets, and even vacuum cleaners may serve as fitness gear. Who knew cleaning items could be used as training equipment?

The Playlist: Create an invigorating playlist with lively music. Consider "Eye of the Tiger" meets "Whistle While You Work." Music will keep everyone engaged and make tasks into exercises seem like a celebration.

Chore-Olympics in Full Swing

Now that you're prepared, it's time to transform chores into a pleasant and productive exercise. Here are some chore-based activities to help you get started:

1. The Vacuum Dash

Description: Make vacuuming a high-energy sprint.
How to Play: Set a two-minute timer. Each player must vacuum as much floor area as possible in the time allotted. Artistic vacuum patterns, such as zigzags, spirals, and happy faces, will get bonus points.
Benefits: This workout boosts heart rate and strengthens arm muscles. Plus, your floors will be the cleanest in town.

2. Laundry Lift-Off

Description: Folding clothes becomes a strength-training exercise.
How To play: Divide the laundry pile equally among players. Each individual must rapidly fold their pile and then rush to put it away. For an added challenge, consider maintaining a plank posture while folding socks.
Benefits: This workout improves arm and core strength. It also teaches important life skills; folding fitted sheets is an art form.

3. The Sweeping Stretch

Description: Sweep your way to flexibility.

How To Play: Extend while sweeping. Reach high, squat low, then do some lunges for good measure. As an added twist, see who can sweep the most dirt into the dustpan without spilling.
Benefits: This workout enhances flexibility and balance. It also guarantees that the corners and baseboards get the attention they need.

4. Duster Dance-Off

Description: Dusting turns into a dancing party.
How to Play: Turn on your favorite songs and dance while cleaning. Encourage freestyle actions like twirls, jumps, and quirky footwork. Have a dance-off to see who can do the greatest moves while removing dust.
Benefits: This activity improves cardiovascular health and coordination. Furthermore, dancing is an excellent approach to improve everyone's mood.

5. Mop Mania

Description: Mopping provides a whole body exercise.
How To Play: Assign each person a piece of the floor to clean. The aim is to clear the area using a variety of maneuvers, including figure eights, side-to-side slides, and a few squats. For extra entertainment, consider synchronized cleaning routines.
Benefits: This action targets the arms, legs, and core. It's like an all-in-one workout, with the additional benefit of gleaming clean floors.

Keeping It Fun and Fresh

To keep the enthusiasm continuing, switch up the duties and obstacles. Here are some other suggestions to make your PE-chore sessions interesting:

Obstacle Course: Create a domestic obstacle course using furniture, pillows, and toys. Include duties in the lesson, such cleaning a shelf or folding a towel. Time each person and see who finishes the course the quickest.

Team Tasks: Participants may work in pairs to complete tasks. For example, one person may hold a board while the other sweeps underneath it. Switch roles to see which team finishes first.

Seasonal Themes: Adapt your PE-chore workouts to the changing seasons or vacations. In the winter, organize a "snow shoveling" race using white paper and a broom. Turn housekeeping into a frightening treasure hunt this Halloween.

Beyond the Basics

After you've mastered the essentials, think about expanding out into more complex jobs.
Organize themed PE days that focus on different types of training or activities. One day may be a "Dance Party Day" with various dance-related tasks, while another could be a "Strength Training Day" with heavy lifting and resistance exercises.

Create family PE activities that combine fun and fitness. Relay races, treasure hunts, and even playing "Twister" at home may make duties more pleasant and physically difficult.

Prioritize outside chores. Gardening, raking leaves, shoveling snow, and washing the car are all great ways to get some physical activity while caring for your home's exterior.

Turning chores into gym class is a wonderful way to keep your kids active, involved, and entertained while still performing some much-needed housework. With a little creativity and a lot of enthusiasm, you can transform everyday tasks into exciting physical education activities that everyone will love.

So, Crazy Homeschool Mama, get your cleaning supplies, put on your favorite music, and begin the PE-chore-olympics. You've got this!

Chapter 22: Field Trips: Turning Grocery Shopping into an Educational Adventure

Field trips are a popular aspect of homeschooling because they enable children to learn away from the traditional classroom environment. But, let's be honest: planning a major field trip to a museum or historical site every week might be daunting. Fear not, Crazy Homeschool Mama, there is a simple solution: turn your ordinary grocery shopping trip into an educational experience! With a little ingenuity and practicality, you may transform the unpleasant chore of grocery shopping into an educational opportunity for your children. Let us begin the process of changing the grocery store into your new school.

The Importance of Everyday Learning

Before getting into the technicalities, let's talk about why daily learning is so important. Routine tasks, such as grocery shopping, are transformed into educational experiences, teaching children that learning is not limited to the classroom or the textbook. It occurs anywhere, at any moment. Grocery shopping has real-world applicability for a wide range of disciplines, making it an excellent field trip activity.

Preparation: Setting the Stage for Learning

Preparation is essential for getting the most of your food shopping excursion. Here's how to prepare:

Goals: Set learning goals for your trip. Exploring cuisine from many cultures might help you improve your arithmetic, nutrition, finance, or geography skills. A defined aim will guide your journey.

Using Shopping Lists as Learning Tools: Include your children in the creation of the shopping list. Younger children may learn writing and spelling, while older children can sort products (fruit, dairy, etc.) and plan meals. It's an excellent technique to get kids interested in the vacation.

Budgeting Basics: Provide each youngster with a tiny budget to manage. They can help you compare pricing and make purchasing selections. It's a practical approach to teaching arithmetic and financial responsibility.

Managing Different School Ages

Children of all ages have diverse learning needs and abilities. Here's how to tailor the supermarket shopping experience to each age group:

Preschoolers:
Engaging the Littlest Learners

Preschoolers are naturally curious and love exploring new environments. Keep their activities simple and fun:

Color Hunt: Conduct a Color and form Hunt by asking students to locate things of a certain color or form. "Can you find anything red?" What about something shaped like a circle?"

Counting Games: Encourage children to count goods as they are added to the cart. "Can you count the number of apples we have?" Now let us add two more!"

Alphabet Adventures: Search for objects beginning with each letter of the alphabet. "What can we find that starts with the letter 'B'?"

Self-Checkout Skills: If your store has self-checkout stations, let your kids take turns scanning items and bagging groceries. It teaches responsibility and basic tech skills.

Elementary School Kids:
Expanding Horizons

Elementary school students can manage more complicated activities and experience a sense of independence:

Math Challenges: Assign easy arithmetic tasks, such as estimating the cost of many things. "If we buy three cans of soup at $1.50 each, how much will that cost?"

Reading Labels: Encourage customers to read product labels and ingredient listings. It's an excellent method to improve your reading skills while also learning more about nutrition.

Cultural exploration: Assign them to discover delicacies from other nations and explore their origins and cultural importance. "Let's find something from Italy and something from Mexico."

Money Management: If you're using cash, let the kids handle the money. They can count out the bills and coins, and even make sure you get the correct change.

Middle Schoolers: Adding Complexity

Middle schoolers are prepared for increasingly complicated duties and responsibilities.

Budgeting and price comparison: Set a budget for a particular area of the shopping list. They may compare costs and decide which goods to purchase. "You have 10 dollars to spend on munchies. "What can you get?"

Nutrition Analysis: Analyze and compare various items' nutritional composition. "Which cereal has more fiber? Which one has less sugar?"

Science in the Aisles: Learn about food preservation, packaging, and storage. "Why do we refrigerate some foods but not others?"

Weight and Measurement: In the produce section, have your kids weigh fruits and vegetables and calculate the cost based on the price per pound. They'll practice using a scale and converting measurements.

High Schoolers: Real-World Applications

High school students can manage intricate work and use critical thinking skills:

Meal Planning and Budgeting: Encourage meal planning, shopping list creation, and money management skills. "Plan a healthy dinner for four people with a $20 budget."

In-Depth Product Analysis: Encourage in-depth product analysis by researching and comparing products based on pricing, ingredients, and ethical practices. "Compare these two brands of coffee. Which one provides more value and is consistent with our values?"

Economic Discussions: Use supermarket trips to examine supply and demand, price changes, and the influence of economic policies on food costs.

Price Comparisons: Challenge your kids to compare prices of different brands and sizes of the same product. Which is the better deal? It's a great way to practice division and understand unit pricing.

Advertising Analysis: Discuss the marketing techniques used on packaging. What words or images are used to make the product appealing? Why might the cereal box have a cartoon character on it?

Making It Fun: Games and Challenges

To make the experience interesting, including some games and challenges in your grocery shopping trip:

Supermarket Bingo: Create bingo cards with items you often buy or see at the grocery store. Each square might represent a particular item or task (such identifying a can of beans, weighing an apple, or finding dairy-free milk). The first person to get bingo wins a little prize.

The Great Grocery Race: Certain a timer and challenge your children to locate all of the goods on the shopping list within a certain time frame. Make careful to highlight the significance of precision over speed; no one wants to return home with pickles instead of cucumbers!

The Alphabet Game: Go around the shop and look for things that begin with each letter of the alphabet. It's an excellent approach to help younger children learn letter recognition while also expanding older children's vocabulary.

Extending the Learning at Home

The educational experience does not have to finish at the supermarket. Extend the learning with activities at home:

Encourage your kids to create their own recipes using the items you purchased. They may prepare a simple meal to share with the family. It's a great approach to improve your writing and creativity.

Encourage your children to keep a nutrition notebook to monitor their food intake and learn about its nutrients. They may create health objectives and assess their eating habits.

The Unexpected Lessons: Embracing the Chaos

No educational journey is complete without a few unexpected lessons.

Patience and flexibility: Stores might be congested, items may be out of stock, or a toddler may have a tantrum in the cereal aisle. These times develop patience and adaptation. Roll with the punches and use the experience to learn about problem-solving.

Social Skills: Grocery shopping provides enough opportunity to develop social skills. Have your children ask shop staff for assistance in locating an item or express gratitude to the cashier. It's an excellent approach to develop confidence and politeness.

Real-World Math: You may need to change your budget or make last-minute choices depending on available resources. These are useful real-world math abilities that textbooks cannot always teach.

Field excursions don't usually include a bus journey or a packed lunch. Sometimes the finest learning opportunities are there in front of us, in the aisles of our neighborhood supermarket. Turning grocery shopping into an educational experience teaches your children that learning is part of daily life and can be enjoyable and exciting.

Chapter 23: Homeschooling on the Road: Turning Travel into an Educational Adventure

Homeschooling provides the unique ability to take learning on the road, turning every journey into a chance for hands-on instruction. Whether you're planning a short road trip or a longer excursion, integrating travel with homeschooling may transform the world into your classroom. In this chapter, we'll look at imaginative methods to include travel into your homeschooling adventure, creating new and exciting learning opportunities for the whole family.

Preparing for a Homeschooling Trip

Proper planning is essential for a successful homeschooling excursion. Here's how to prepare:

Research and Plan: Learn about educational possibilities in your location. Look for museums, historical sites, wildlife reserves, and cultural events that relate to your curriculum. Plan your trip around these fascinating activities.

Pack smartly: Pack the necessary homeschooling resources, but keep them light and portable. Consider workbooks, iPads filled with instructional programs, and your favorite literature. Don't forget the basics, including pencils, notebooks, and a portable whiteboard.

Mobile Learning Kit: Create a mobile learning kit using small and adaptable tools. Include tools such as flashcards, a portable microscope, binoculars, and painting supplies. This package is ideal for spontaneous learning sessions on the fly.

Utilize digital resources: Load up on e-books, instructional applications, and online courses that are accessible from anywhere. A stable internet connection is your greatest buddy for accessing a multitude of information.

Integrating Learning into Travel

Teach geography via travel: Study maps, plan your journey, and learn about your destination's physical and cultural landscape. Discuss landmarks, climate, and ecosystems as you see them.

History Exploration: Explore the history of the areas you visit. Explore historic sites, battles, and museums. Discuss the historical importance and anecdotes surrounding these locations, making each visit a live history lesson.

Cultural Immersion: Expose your family to the local culture. Attend cultural events, explore local markets, and sample ethnic food. Learn a few words in the local tongue and discover the traditions and customs. This firsthand cultural knowledge is vital.

Science in Nature: Nature provides many opportunity for scientific inquiry. Explore national parks, botanical gardens, and animal sanctuaries. To have direct experience with ecosystems, study local flora and wildlife, do small experiments, and go on nature walks.

Creative Travel Activities

Keep learning enjoyable and interesting with these unique vacation activities:

Encourage your children to maintain travel diaries. They may record their experiences, create drawings, and write about what they have learnt. It's an excellent method to improve your writing abilities while also creating a keepsake from your vacation.

Organize scavenger hunts based on your trips. Make a list of things or landmarks to locate and tick off.

This exercise keeps children interested and focused, transforming touring into an enjoyable game.

Give your children cameras and encourage them to make their own projects. They may photograph intriguing sites, chronicle animals, or compile a photo essay about their experience. It's a great method to improve your photography and observation ability.

Seek out local experts or advisors to enhance your understanding. Whether it's a park ranger, museum curator, or local artist, these specialists may provide extensive information and unique perspectives.

Balancing Education and Fun

A successful homeschooling vacation requires striking a mix between organized instruction and spontaneous enjoyment.

Maintain a flexible schedule to accommodate planned educational activities and spontaneous discovery. Some of the finest learning situations are unexpected.

Allow enough time for recreation and relaxation. Travel may be exhausting, and everyone needs relaxation. Visit playgrounds, beaches, or just have a relaxing picnic.

Engage in family talks throughout trip. Reflect on what you've seen and learned, share your ideas and views, and encourage open-ended inquiries. These talks help to increase understanding and strengthen family bonds.

Turn meals into learning opportunities. Try local cuisines, talk about the ingredients and preparation processes, and discover the cultural importance of certain meals. Cooking together may also be an enjoyable and instructive experience.

Managing Challenges on the Road

Traveling while homeschooling has its own set of obstacles. Here's how to handle them:

Staying Organized: Organize your homeschooling materials and travel requirements. Stay organized with packing cubes, labeled bags, and digital organizing tools.

Dealing with Disruptions: Prepare for interruptions, such as severe weather, delays, or unexpected closures. Have backup plans and other activities ready to go. Flexibility is your most valuable asset.

Health and Safety: Prioritize health and safety throughout travel. Carry a first-aid kit, remain hydrated, and adhere to local health requirements. Ensure that everyone understands fundamental safety guidelines for new surroundings.

Maintaining Consistency: While flexibility is necessary, having some consistency may give stability.

Maintain a few regular habits, such as morning reading or nighttime meditations, to help anchor your days.

Learning Through Service

Integrate service learning into your trips to educate empathy and community participation.

Look for volunteer opportunities around your location. Participate in neighborhood clean-ups, visit animal shelters, or volunteer at local food banks. These exercises provide vital life lessons and have a good influence.

Conduct cultural exchange activities. Connect with local families or community organizations to learn about their lives and share your own. This promotes mutual understanding and respect.

Practice environmental responsibility by contributing to conservation activities. Beach clean-ups, tree planting, and animal preservation are all activities that foster a feeling of environmental responsibility.

Documenting Your Journey

Keeping a diary of your trip homeschooling experiences is both informative and enjoyable:

Travel Blog or Vlog: Create a family trip blog or vlog. Document your experiences, share what you've learnt, and reflect on your journey.

It's an excellent approach to improve your writing, video editing, and digital communication abilities.

Scrapbooking: Create a scrapbook with souvenirs, photographs, and keepsakes from your trips. This hands-on craft is a unique way to remember your travel and reflect on your experiences.

Family Presentations: At the conclusion of the vacation, ask each family member to produce a presentation about their favorite portion. This might be a slide display, a written report, or even a little movie. It's an excellent approach to reinforce learning and share memories.

Homeschooling on the road is an excellent way to convert travel into a valuable educational experience. You may create amazing excursions that enrich your homeschooling journey by planning ahead of time, including learning into your journey, balancing education and enjoyment, and efficiently handling problems.

Remember that the world is your school, and there is so much to learn outside the confines of your house.

Chapter 24: Grading and Assessments: Yes, You Can Test Without Tears

Ah, evaluations and progress monitoring. Even the most experienced homeschooling parent may get chills down his or her spine after hearing those words. But don't worry, fellow crazy homeschool mother, this chapter is here to assist you navigate the sometimes murky seas of assessing success without losing your head (or sanity). Remember that in the world of homeschooling, progress is not always a straight line.

Why Assessments Matter

First, let's discuss why evaluations are important. It's not only about ticking off boxes and completing report cards. Assessments enable you to understand where your kid is in their learning journey, identify strengths and areas for progress, and ensure you're on the right road. Plus, they provide you with something tangible to show skeptical relatives who still believe "homeschooling" implies "watching TV all day."

Types of Assessments

There are numerous evaluations you may use to track your child's growth. Here is a list of the most prevalent ones:

Standardized tests: These are the ones we all remember (or fear) from our school days. They are helpful for comparing your child's performance to national standards, but they are not the end-all of evaluation.

Informal assessments: They include observations, talks, and daily contacts. They're ideal for assessing your child's comprehension in a relaxed setting. Furthermore, they do not need any bubble sheets or number 2 pencils.

Portfolios: A portfolio showcases your child's work over time. Essays, art projects, quizzes, and other types of assignments may be included. Portfolios provide a comprehensive perspective of growth and may be an enjoyable method to highlight your child's accomplishments. It's similar to scrapbooking, but with more instructional substance and less glitter (unless you like that).

Narrative Assessments: This type provides extensive written explanations of your child's growth. They're excellent at catching the intricacies of learning that standardized examinations may overlook. Consider them the "Dear Diary" entries of the homeschooling community.

Self-Assessment: Help your kid reflect on their own learning and establish objectives for progress. This not only encourages kids to take control of their education, but it also offers you with vital information. Plus, it's always fascinating to watch how your youngster perceives their own improvement; occasionally they surprise you!

Using Standardized Tests Without Stress

Standardized exams may be informative, but they can also be stressful. Here's how to utilize them without blowing your mind:

Select the appropriate test. Homeschoolers may choose from a variety of standardized assessments. Research your alternatives and choose one that is consistent with your educational philosophy and your child's requirements. Popular options include the Iowa Test of Basic Skills (ITBS) and the Stanford Achievement Test.

Help your kid prepare for the exam without making it a stressful affair. Practice exams, review sessions, and a calm, helpful attitude may all help. Remember that this is just one measure of development.

Remember that test results are not the only factor to consider. Use them as a tool for understanding, not as a conclusive assessment of your child's talents or homeschooling success. If your child's score is lower than anticipated, it is a chance to find areas for improvement, not a reason for alarm.

Making Informal Assessments Fun

Informal evaluations allow you to fully express your creative, wacky homeschool mother side. Here are some entertaining methods to evaluate your child's progress:

Observation: Observe your child's approach to various chores and topics. Are they interested and curious?

Do they ask questions and form connections? These observations may provide useful insights regarding their learning.

Discussions: Regularly discuss what your youngster is learning. Ask open-ended inquiries and encourage them to clarify things in their own terms. Bonus points if you do this with a bowl of popcorn or on a family stroll.

Learning Games: Use educational games to test your child's knowledge in a fun and engaging manner. Board games, card games, and internet games may all be valuable resources. Just be prepared for some friendly rivalry, and maybe some gloating from the winner.

Projects and Presentations: Encourage your youngster to apply their knowledge via assignments. A scientific experiment, a history lecture, or an art project are all examples of hands-on activities that might show comprehension.

Reading Aloud: Encourage your youngster to read aloud to you frequently. This allows you to measure their reading abilities while also providing a chance to discuss the content together. Plus, it's an excellent excuse to curl up with a nice book.

Creating and Maintaining Portfolios

Portfolios are an excellent tool to chronicle and highlight your child's development throughout time. Here's how to construct and keep one without becoming a hoarder:

Select a format. Choose between a physical portfolio (e.g., binder or scrapbook) and a digital portfolio (e.g., website or folder). Both offer benefits, so select the one that best suits your needs.

Gather work examples showing your child's improvement in many topics. This may contain written tasks, artwork, project images, and more. Try to create a balance between displaying their greatest work and charting their progress.

Organize the portfolio by topic or theme for simple navigation. You may also build sections for various school years to demonstrate growth over time.

Encourage your youngster to write thoughts on their work. What did they enjoy? What did they find challenging? What are they proud of? These thoughts provide richness to the portfolio and shed light on their learning journey.

Schedule frequent portfolio reviews and updates. This keeps it manageable and ensures that it correctly represents your child's growth. It also provides an excellent chance for them to celebrate their accomplishments together.

Narrative Assessments: Telling the Story of Learning

Narrative evaluations provide a deep, qualitative look at your child's development. Here's how to compose them without feeling like you're in school again:

Take thorough notes on your child's learning progress, triumphs, and obstacles throughout the year. This will make composing the narrative evaluation a lot simpler.

Provide concrete instances to demonstrate your child's improvement. Instead of declaring, "Johnny is good at math," use the phrase, "Johnny has mastered multiplication and is now working on division with confidence."

Balance your appraisal by highlighting strengths and areas for growth. Highlight your child's strengths and successes, while simultaneously identifying opportunities for improvement.

Use quotes and stories to bring personality and context to your narrative evaluation. Include memorable incidents and hilarious anecdotes to make the evaluation more interesting.

Encourage your youngster by focusing on the good parts of their learning path. Use constructive comments to help them progress, but always in a kind and supportive tone.

Involving Your Child in Self-Assessments

Self-assessment is an effective strategy for developing independence and self-awareness. Here's how to engage your toddler in the process.

Establish common learning objectives at the start of each term or year. This instills in your youngster a feeling of responsibility and direction.

Schedule frequent check-ins to discuss progress towards objectives. Encourage your kid to think about what is going well and what they may need assistance with.

Utilize Self-Assessment Tools: Use checklists, reflection diaries, and progress charts to help your kid monitor their own learning. These methods may help make self-evaluation more tangible and manageable.

Celebrate your child's triumphs and milestones. Whether it's a high-five, a special reward, or a fun excursion, praising their accomplishments encourages healthy learning habits.

Promote a development mentality by valuing effort and endurance above perfection. Encourage your youngster to see problems as chances to develop.

Creative Assessment Ideas

Let's look at some innovative evaluation ideas that will make the process more pleasurable for both you and your youngster.

Learning Journals: Encourage your kid to start a learning notebook to reflect on their daily or weekly experiences. They can draw drawings, write summaries, and even make comic strips. This not only helps kids digest their information, but it also makes a lovely souvenir to look back on.

Photo Essays: Create picture essays to chronicle your child's projects and learning experiences.

Create picture essays that capture the tale of their learning experiences. This is very enjoyable for visual learners and creates a stunning visual record of their progress.

Learning Fairs: Organize a learning fair at home to showcase your child's work and accomplishments to the family. They may put up exhibits, provide presentations, and field queries. It's similar to a scientific fair, but with less pressure and more family fun.

Video Diaries: Encourage your kid to produce video diaries to share their learning, show abilities, and give mini-lessons. This is an excellent method to evaluate your speaking and presenting abilities, and it can be a lot of fun to watch together.

Interactive Notebooks: Enable your youngster to add foldables, drawings, charts, and other interactive components. These notebooks may be used for any topic and provide a hands-on approach to monitor learning.

Incorporating Humor and Fun

As a crazy homeschool mother, you understand that comedy and fun are critical components of a successful homeschooling experience. Here are some strategies to make exams more enjoyable and humorous:
Provide amusing commentary on your child's efforts. For example, "Great job on your dinosaur essay!" I believe T-Rex would give you a thumbs up if he could."

Celebrate your child's accomplishments via goofy rituals. Perhaps you have a "dance party" every time they learn a new ability, or a "hat day" when everyone wears a goofy hat to commemorate a milestone.

Begin each evaluation session with a joke to lighten the atmosphere. Something like, "Why did the math book seem sad? Because it has a lot of difficulties!" A little humor may go a long way toward reducing stress.

Create innovative trophies to recognize various achievements. What about the "Master of Multiplication" or "Reading Rockstar"? Make the awards bright and entertaining, and deliver them with much fanfare.

Dealing with Setbacks and Challenges

Even with the greatest plans and intentions, there will be setbacks and obstacles.

Accept that not every day will be ideal. There will be days when the dog eats your schoolwork (literally), or the scientific experiment transforms the kitchen into a disaster zone. Accept flaws and use them as learning opportunities.

Be adaptable. Be open to adjust your strategy if it's not working. One of the most significant benefits of homeschooling is its flexibility, so take use of it. If you feel that the curriculum is pulling you down, it may be time to change things up.

Prioritize Progress Over Perfection. Focus on making progress rather than achieving perfection. Celebrate modest successes and progress, even if they aren't great leaps. Every little of improvement is worth recognizing.

Take breaks as needed. If you or your kid are feeling overwhelmed, take a break. Taking a break from time to time might bring a new perspective and energy. Breaks are not a sign of failure, but rather an important aspect of preserving balance and sanity.

Homeschooling development and success may be an enjoyable, creative, and meaningful endeavor. You may assist your child's learning journey without losing your mind by employing a range of evaluation techniques, including humor and enjoyment, and being adaptable and optimistic. Remember, the objective is to instill a love of learning in your kid and to enjoy your unique path together.

Chapter 25: Celebrating Success: Rewarding the Small Victories

In the crazy world of homeschooling, it's easy to get engrossed in the daily grind of lesson plans, arithmetic problems, and the never-ending search for the misplaced glue stick. However, in the middle of the bustle, it is important to take a break and celebrate tiny achievements. These are the moments that make homeschooling gratifying and keep everyone motivated, even if the greatest accomplishment of the day is not losing your sanity by midday. So, let's plunge into the delicious art of homeschooling success!

Recognizing the Small Wins

Every day in homeschooling is full with little accomplishments that ought to be celebrated. Here's how to recognize and appreciate tiny wins:

Mastering a New Skill: Celebrate with a victory dance when your youngster masters a new skill, such as long division or spelling "supercalifragilisticexpialidocious". And yeah, you should totally participate - additional points for moonwalking.

Completing a Project: Completing a project, whether it's a science fair volcano that didn't erupt on the cat or a history presentation performed with Oscar-worthy zeal, is an accomplishment. Break out the party munchies and let your youngster to soak in the joy of their achievement.

Surviving the Day: Sometimes the greatest achievement is just getting through the day without a dramatic breakdown (from yourself or your children). These days call for a round of applause, an extra cookie, and maybe a lengthy bath in the tub with the door shut.

Random Acts of Kindness: Celebrate your child's random acts of kindness, such as helping a sibling with schoolwork or setting the table without being asked. These are pure gold moments that need to be recognized, maybe with a "Kindness Champion" plaque fashioned of glitter and macaroni.

Creative Ways to Celebrate

Celebrating accomplishment does not have to include having a party. Here are some fun and inventive ways to celebrate your modest victories:

Sticker Charts: Don't underestimate the impact of a visually appealing sticker. Create a chart where your youngster may place a sticker for each accomplishment. Allow them to select a little reward when they reach a specific amount, such as which movie to watch for family night or what to eat for dinner (hopefully not ice cream and ketchup).

Treasure box: Fill a box with modest and cheap snacks or toys. Every time your kid reaches a milestone, they may choose anything from the treasure box. Pro tip: Fill it with items you secretly desire, such as the small packs of gummy bears you've been admiring.

Certificates of Awesomeness: Print certificates of awesomeness for accomplishments such as "Reading Rockstar" or "Math Magician." Present them with all the pomp and grandeur you can conjure, including trumpets, a red carpet, and a sincere speech praising their greatness.

DIY Medals: Make DIY medals using ribbon and glittering materials (e.g., foil, buttons, keys). Award them for outstanding accomplishments and let your youngster walk about like the homeschool Olympian they are.

Special Outings: Celebrate significant milestones with a memorable excursion. This may include a visit to the zoo, an ice cream shop, or a day in the park. It's an excellent method to recognize work and create lasting memories.

Incorporating Fun Traditions

Traditions provide enthusiasm and expectation to your homeschooling routine. Here are some enjoyable methods to make festivities a regular feature of your homeschool:

Fabulous Friday: Designate Fridays as "Fabulous Friday" and celebrate the week's successes. Play games, have a dance party, or indulge in a unique treat. It's a terrific way to conclude the week on a positive note and give everyone something to look forward to.

Shout-out Jar: Create a "Shout-Out Jar" where family members may leave messages to acknowledge one other's efforts and accomplishments. Read them aloud after dinner or a family meeting, and don't forget to offer kudos to the individual who told the funniest joke that week!

Victory Songs: Create a family victory song to celebrate major accomplishments. Whether it's a customized chant or a funny song, celebrating accomplishment can be a fun and unforgettable experience. Simply be prepared for unplanned performances in the middle of the grocery store.

Achievement Wall: Create a wall or bulletin board to display accomplishments. Display artwork, diplomas, and images from finished projects. It serves as a visible reminder of your child's efforts and a fantastic discussion starter for guests ("Wow, I didn't know you were an expert on Ancient Egyptian mummies!").

Celebrating Yourself

Let us not forget about you, the intrepid homeschool parent. You, too, deserve to celebrate your own accomplishments, because, let's be honest, keeping the ship afloat is a worthy accomplishment. Here's how you can pamper yourself.

Reward yourself with a luxury coffee break. Enjoy a nice cappuccino or your favorite tea while celebrating a well-taught lesson or a day when no one sobbed over math.

Solo outings Plan some solitary adventures for yourself. Whether it's a peaceful stroll in the park, a visit to your favorite bookshop, or a lengthy bath with a good book, making time for yourself is a win worth celebrating.

Create a "Parent Brag Board" to highlight your personal achievements, such as "Survived the Great Glue Spill of '24" or "Taught Algebra Without Crying." It's a pleasant method to recognize your efforts and remind yourself that you're doing an excellent job at homeschooling.

Declare "Treat Yourself Day" periodically. Order takeout, binge-watch your favorite program, or purchase that item you've been admiring. Because sometimes the greatest way to celebrate is to do some self-care.

Celebrating little achievements in homeschooling is critical for keeping everyone motivated and the experience pleasurable. Every accomplishment, whether it's mastering a difficult topic, completing a large assignment, or just getting through the day, deserves to be celebrated. So, pull out the stickers, medals, and victory songs - and remember that it's all about the little victories along the journey, not just the big ones.

Chapter 26: Handling Setbacks: When Your Lesson Plan Explodes

Homeschooling is an adventure full of twists, turns, and unexpected surprises – kind of like trying to assemble IKEA furniture without the instructions. Just when you think you've got everything under control, life throws a curveball, and your perfectly planned lesson on the American Revolution somehow ends up in a heated debate about who ate the last cookie. Even the best-laid plans can explode in a cloud of glitter and confusion.

Embracing the Chaos

Let's face it: setbacks are unavoidable. Here's how to accept the chaos and ride with it:

Lower Expectations: Setting unrealistic expectations might lead to disappointment throughout the day. Instead, set a reasonable objective, such as going through algebra without weeping (including yourself).

Plan B, C, and D: Always have a backup plan (or three). When the scientific experiment fails and your history lecture is interrupted by an impromptu dance-off, you'll be pleased you have some additional activities on hand.

Flexibility is your best friend, much like that extra bag of cookies stashed in the cabinet for emergencies.

Just Laugh: When things go wrong, laugh it off. It's hard to be irritated when you're laughing about how your effort to teach fractions evolved into a full-fledged flour war. Remember, laughing is the greatest medicine, and it's free of calories!

The Great Experiment Fail

Ah, the excitement of hands-on learning - and the occasional terror when your hands-on lesson gets out of hand. Here's how to handle experiment failures with flair:

Before you begin any scientific project, ensure that you have enough safety precautions in place. Goggles, gloves, and a fire extinguisher are ideal starting points. Always maintain a cleaning plan on hand. You never know when the "harmless" vinegar and baking soda volcano may erupt into Mount Vesuvius.

Document the failure and use it as a learning opportunity. Take photographs, make notes, and ask your children what they believe happened wrong. Not only is this an excellent technique to teach scientific thinking, but it also creates amusing memories. Future science courses will struggle to surpass the moment your homemade rocket repainted the ceiling.

Celebrate the effort, even if the experiment did not proceed as expected.

Give out "Mad Scientist" trophies or "Captain Cleanup" medals to anyone who assisted with the aftermath. Because, well, cleaning up after an indoor snowfall of cornstarch deserves some real credit.

The Lesson That Went Off the Rails

Sometimes a lesson plan takes an unexpected turn and you end yourself teaching a whole other topic. Here's how to get things back on track without losing your cool.

Embrace the unexpected: If your ancient Egypt lesson turns into a conversation about aliens creating the pyramids, go with it. Ask questions, research the subject, and see where it goes. You may find a new interest or viewpoint, or you may just giggle at the absurdity of it all.

Refocus and redirect: When the talk becomes risky or outrageously off-topic, gently redirect it back. Use sentences such as "That's interesting!" How about we complete this and return to it later?" It's like herding cats with a forceful but soft hand.

Turn It into a Game: Make getting back on track enjoyable by turning it into a game. Challenge your students to discover a method to connect the current subject to the original lesson. It's like a mental treasure hunt, and it may save your sanity.

The Technology Tantrum

Technology may be a homeschooler's greatest friend—until it chooses to throw a fit. Here's what to do when your technology goes rogue:

Technical Troubleshooting 101: Learn basic troubleshooting. When your laptop stalls or the Wi-Fi goes down, having a few techniques under your sleeve may save the day. If everything else fails, switch it off and back on - that solves 90% of technical issues.

Screen-free backups: Always have screen-free activities on hand in case technology fails. Get out a board game, some painting equipment, or go outdoors for an impromptu nature lesson. Sometimes the best option is to go old school, and you may even discover that you appreciate the vacation from screens.

Laugh at Glitches: When the computer chooses to update in the midst of a class or the printer begins printing blank pages, it's easy to get upset. Instead, attempt to find comedy in the circumstance. After all, who knew a paper jam could result in such a stunning collection of contemporary art?

Setbacks are an unavoidable aspect of homeschooling, but they do not have to ruin your day. With a little flexibility, a healthy dose of humor, and a willingness to roll with the punches, even the most spectacular calamities may be turned into learning experiences and unforgettable memories. Remember that the goal is not to avoid setbacks, but to embrace them and discover the silver lining.

Chapter 27:
The Day You Decide to Stop Homeschooling and Join the School Bus Brigade

So, Crazy Homeschool Mama, you've had a great run. However, the moment has come to contemplate what was once unthinkable: sending your children to conventional schools. Making the changeover may be both terrifying and funny, depending on life events, your child's changing requirements, or the urgent need for a minute of calm. Let's start our new adventure with a grin and a chuckle.

The Decision-Making Process

The decision to abandon homeschooling and return to formal school is typically accompanied by feelings of relief, remorse, and a weird sense of liberation. Here's how to make this important choice without losing your mind.

The Aha Moment: Had a "Aha!" moment when explaining trigonometry to a kid who was painting the dog blue? Perhaps it was the sixth breakdown of the day, and it was just you. Whatever the reason, you recognize that it is time for a change. "Oh my gosh, they need to go to school," you think to yourself, and the choice is made.

The Guilt Trip: Feel the guilt. Are you giving up? Are you failing them? Take a deep breath and know that every parent has these emotions. You aren't failing; you're adjusting. If conventional education is what your family needs right now, it is the best option.

Pros and cons list: Write out the advantages and disadvantages. Advantages: More personal time, socializing for the children, and someone else teaching mathematics. Cons: Lunch preparation, PTA meetings, and the terror of early morning drop-offs. The professionals are beginning to look nice, right?

The Big Announcement

Telling your children that they will be attending regular school may be a big deal. Expect a wide variety of emotions, from ecstatic to dramatic tears.

The Enthusiast: There's usually one youngster who is ecstatic about the notion. "I get to take the bus? With other children? "Sign me up!" Their enthusiasm is infectious, and you begin to feel better about the entire situation.

The Drama Queen or King: Then there's the one who behaves as if you've revealed they're relocating to Siberia. "What do you mean, school?" With instructors and other students? "Today is the worst day of my life!" Stay calm and explain all the beautiful aspects of school, such as recess and pizza day.

The Indifferent One: Finally, there's the child who just shrugs. "Cool. Can I continue playing video games after school?" Their lack of emotion is strangely soothing. At least someone is taking it with stride.

Preparing for the Big Day

The move from homeschooling to formal schooling needs planning and a sense of humor. Here's how to prepare without losing your calm.

School Supplies Shopping: Shopping for school supplies might seem like a competition. Lists, crowds, and a frenzied search for the last pack of colored pencils. Accept the pandemonium and reward yourself with a coffee (or something stronger) afterwards. Pro tip: Let the kids choose a fun backpack. It's a little detail, but it helps get people psyched.

New wardrobe: If your kids have been living in pajamas and superhero costumes, it's time to improve their clothing. Shop in-store or online for school-appropriate clothing. Just try not to faint at the checkout when you see how much a pair of pants costs.

Early morning drills: Begin adapting to the new schedule by practicing early wake-ups. This is when you realize how much you've taken for granted those relaxing homeschool mornings. Set alarms, prepare breakfast, and pretend it's school day. It's like boot camp, just with more cereal spills.

The First Day of School

The big day comes. Your emotions are all over the place, but you can handle it. Here's how to manage it:

School parking lot is a combat zone. You negotiate the mayhem, eventually finding a parking place, and giving your children a pep talk. They may be apprehensive, but they are prepared, as are you.

As you watch them go inside the school building, you feel pride, relief, and maybe grief. You've done an excellent job homeschooling, and it's time for a new experience. Once they're out of sight, you may even perform a joyful dance back to your vehicle. It's OK, no one is watching.

When you get home, it's suddenly silent. Too quiet. Enjoy the solitude for a bit, then realize you can finally clean without someone wrecking your effort right away. Or take a sleep. Napping is excellent.

Chapter 28: Graduation Day: Looking Back on the Journey

Congratulations, Crazy Homeschool Mama and Dad! You made it to graduation day. Whether you're in kindergarten, high school, or anywhere in between, it's time to put on your handmade hats, throw some confetti, and reflect on the crazy, funny, and wonderful adventure that led you here. This chapter is about celebrating your successes, laughing at your mistakes, and cherishing every minute of your homeschooling journey. So, gather your Kleenex (and maybe a glass of celebratory bubbly), and let's go down memory lane.

The First Day Fiasco

Remember the very first day of homeschooling? You had big intentions and a properly color-coded itinerary. What's the reality? Let's just say it was more of a "learn as you go" experience.

The Morning Meltdown: You had planned a great start with breakfast, a pep talk, and lessons. Instead, you had a complete tantrum because someone couldn't locate their favorite pencil. Welcome to homeschooling, where locating a lost pencil may seem like a high-stakes treasure hunt.

The Tech Tangle: You thought you'd start with some nice internet resources. Instead, you spent two hours untangling cords and determining why the Wi-Fi refused to cooperate. By the time you had everything operating, it was lunchtime, and you hadn't even begun the first session.

The Cat Cameo: During your well-planned "Welcome to Homeschool" speech, the cat chose to swagger across the table and sit on the lesson plan. The youngsters found it amusing, and you soon learned to roll with the punches.

The Mid-Year Madness

Around mid-year, you found your groove - or at least worked out how to balance lesson preparations, cleaning, and the odd existential crisis.

The Great Science Experiment: Have you ever accidentally caused a little explosion in the kitchen while demonstrating a basic chemical reaction? The students were excited, the cat was terrified, and you included "unexpected science" into your lesson plan.

Field Trip Fiasco: You had planned an instructive field trip to the museum, but instead spent the most of the day looking for a restroom. What's the highlight? The unexpected education in antique plumbing systems and a renewed respect for contemporary amenities.

The Art Attack: An out-of-control art project transformed the living room into a contemporary installation. You realized that glitter is the herpes of the craft industry; it never goes away. But hey, the kids learnt about texture, and you learned how to put up art projects outside.

The Graduation Ceremony

And here we are on graduation day. It's time to celebrate all of your hard work, laughing, and learning that has led you to this point.

Create a DIY diploma with construction paper and glitter (if you dare). It may not be official, but it represents your passion and love for homeschooling.

Graduation is incomplete without the cap and gown. Whether you make one out of old bedsheets or buy a little one online, it's the ideal way to commemorate this occasion. Don't forget to take plenty of photographs; you'll want to remember this day.

Give a sincere speech that includes both emotional and amusing remarks. Remind your youngster of their wonderful accomplishments and how pleased you are of their path. Don't forget to thank the cat for its steadfast (and sometimes disruptive) support.

Graduation Day is a celebration of the journey, including the highs and lows.

As you fling those hats in the air and maybe shed a tear or two, keep in mind that homeschooling is about more than simply academics. It's about instilling a love of learning, encouraging curiosity, and forming a strong, supporting family tie.

So, here's to you, Crazy Homeschool Mama (and Dad): you did an excellent job.
Continue enjoying, learning, and cherishing every minute of this great trip. You have earned it!

Chapter 29: What You Learn from This Homeschool Journey

Congratulations, Crazy Homeschool Mama! You've reached the end of this homeschooling journey. As you reflect on the voyage, take time to consider the lessons gained, the development you've experienced, and the innumerable memories you've built along the road. Homeschooling is more than simply education; it's a way of life, full of ups and downs. So, regardless of whether you're a working mom, a member of a busy family, or a single superhero mom managing kids of all ages, let's delve into what you've learnt from this great journey.

The Art of Patience

Homeschooling teaches patience in ways you never imagined possible. Whether you're teaching math for the hundredth time or coping with the umpteenth interruption during a history class, you've mastered the art of patience. You've learned to take deep breaths, grin through the noise, and remember that learning is a process, not a competition. Consider yourself a zen master if you can remain cool throughout a tantrum from a toddler while on a conference call.

The Beauty of Flexibility

If homeschooling has taught you one thing, it's the value of flexibility. Plans change, lessons derail, and you sometimes have to roll with the punches. You've learned to adjust on the fly, transforming unexpected events into important learning experiences. Snow day? Ideal for a quick scientific lecture on snowflakes. Is the Internet down? It's time for an old-school book and some comfortable reading time. Whether you're juggling business commitments, family obligations, or just keeping everyone amused, flexibility has become your strength.

The Value of Time Saved

No more early rushes or driving for hours on end. Homeschooling has saved you a lot of time and energy. No more frantic hunts for misplaced shoes or the stress of getting to the bus station on time.

Those additional hours have been regained for productive study, family togetherness, and maybe a few more minutes of sleep. As a working mother, every minute saved on the road means extra time for a well-deserved coffee break.

The Financial Wins

Let us not overlook the money saved. Homeschooling eliminates tuition costs, pricey uniforms, and constant fundraising. You've put your money towards educational materials, engaging experiences, and maybe a well-deserved family trip. You've also honed your skills in discovering cost-effective methods to improve your child's educational experience. Whether you're a single mother pushing every dollar or part of a dual-income family, those savings have made a significant impact.

The Joy of Learning Together

One of the most valuable benefits of homeschooling is the ability to learn with your children. You've rediscovered things you hadn't considered in years, and you've shared the excitement of discovery with your children. You've felt the excitement of learning as a family, whether it was a fascinating historical event, a complicated scientific subject, or a beautiful work of literature. The delight of shared learning is universal, whether your family is tiny or large.

The Strength of Family Bonds

Homeschooling has improved your family relationships in ways you never expected. You've spent many hours together, navigating the ups and downs of school and life. Your family has grown closer through shared achievements and tribulations, fostering a strong feeling of trust, understanding, and love. These ties are the cornerstone of your homeschooling experience and the treasure you will bring with you. Whether you parent alone or with a spouse, those relationships are unbreakable.

The Power of Creativity

You've learned to look beyond the box, transforming ordinary situations into learning opportunities. You've converted your house into a dynamic learning environment, with the kitchen functioning as a scientific lab and the backyard serving as a classroom. Your imagination has transformed monotonous jobs into intriguing lessons, and you've discovered pleasure in the process of making learning enjoyable and exciting. Whether you're brainstorming classes over a lunch break or preparing activities while cooking supper, your imagination has no limitations.

The Importance of Self-Care

You've learnt the value of self-care while homeschooling. You've realized that a well-rested and happy mother is necessary for a successful homeschool.

Whether it's a calm cup of coffee in the morning, a quick stroll in the afternoon, or a well-deserved siesta, self-care has become an essential part of your daily routine. Finding time for yourself is essential, no matter how hectic your day is.

The Wisdom of Community

You recognize the benefits of a supporting community. From local homeschool organizations to internet forums, you've discovered a community of like-minded parents who understand your pleasures and frustrations. These relationships have offered you counsel, support, and a feeling of community. You've learned that you're never alone on this road, and help is just a phone call or click away. Whether you're a member of a thriving homeschool co-op or a virtual support group, community makes a huge impact.

The Humor in the Chaos

Perhaps the most essential lesson is how to find comedy in the midst of turmoil. Homeschooling is full of unexpected moments, and you've learned to laugh at the mistakes and accept the flaws. Whether it's a toddler's "artwork" on the wall, a cat photobombing a Zoom lesson, or a scientific project gone horribly wrong, you've discovered that laughing is the greatest way to get through the ups and downs. Your sense of humor has been your saving grace, whether you're dealing with one kid or a full family.

Embracing the Journey

As you reflect on your homeschooling adventure, keep in mind that the trip is just as important as the goal. Every day, every lesson, and every obstacle has formed you and your children in significant ways. You've developed a one-of-a-kind educational experience that combines love, fun, and learning. Regardless of your position, the voyage was worthwhile.

Homeschooling is a unique experience, with teachings that go well beyond academics. You've learnt patience, adaptability, inventiveness, and the value of self-care. You've built family relationships, saved time and money, and enjoyed the process of learning together. Most significantly, you've realized the importance of comedy and a supporting group.

As you end this chapter, know that you did an excellent job. You've handled the crazy world of homeschooling with grace, resilience, and plenty of laughs. The lessons you've learned will remain with you and your children for the rest of your lives, influencing who you are and will become.

So, here's to you, Crazy Homeschool Mama: whether you work, are part of a busy family, or are a single superhero mom, you've done it, and you're an example to all of us!

Printed in Dunstable, United Kingdom

65299653R00097